How to Write
and Sell a
Christian Novel

How to Write and Sell a Christian Novel

GILBERT MORRIS

WRITE NOW!

Write Now Publications
Phoenix, Arizona 85013

Published by Write Now Publications
A royalty division of ACW Press
5501 N. 7th. Ave., #502,
Phoenix, Arizona 85013
1-800-931-2665
www.acwpress.com

Printed in the United States of America
ISBN 1-892525-17-8

Contents

Introduction

~

How to Use This Book

When people find out that I write novels, they inevitably ask: "How do you write books?"

Would these same questioners ask a pianist, "How do you play the piano?"

Or a surgeon: "How do you perform an operation?"

Or an athlete: "How do you play ball?"

When people are asked, "Can you write?" they often say, "I don't know; I've never tried." But when you ask these same people if they can play the cello, they don't say, "I don't know; I never tried."

The implication here is that most people believe *anyone* can write—and in one sense this is true. If the word *write* means to put meaningful marks on paper (such as a note asking a roommate to put the top back on the toothpaste), any person who has mastered the art of spelling and the act of putting symbols on paper can write.

However, the writing of a novel is based on the understanding of a sharply defined set of principles, and only those who understand these principles can connect the very best words to produce a good novel. You can give a monkey a brush, some paint, and a piece of canvas. You can train the monkey to smear the paint on the canvas. But you couldn't call the monkey's artistic attempt a painting. Because you can't teach a monkey the *principles* of the art of painting.

Someone might say: "Oh, but a seal can be taught to play a tune on a set of horns." Ah, but when prodded to play another tune, it soon becomes obvious that the seal can only play by rote.

In this book you will discover the answers to two important questions:

1. What are the *principles* of writing a novel?
2. How do I build these principles into my work?

If you learn the first (and the principles are easily learned) but not the second, your novel will contain the amateurish flaws that editors spot instantly. Your precious manuscript will end up in a special stack marked RETURN. On the other hand, if you learn the first, and are able to accomplish the second, you will achieve success at novel writing.

In this book, I will give you the principles. But more importantly, I will teach you how to *use* these principles in your writing.

Learning the principles of novel writing is a lot like learning to drive a car. Those of us who learned to drive in a vehicle with a standard shift discovered right away that we couldn't concentrate on two things at once. We may have practiced several skills at the same time, but we could not do them all well at the same time. Not when we first started. *Let's see—turn on the engine—no, take the car out of gear—now step on the clutch—ahh, good!—now put the car in first—let up on the clutch—ooohhh, the car is dying—step on the gas!—now step on the clutch, pull shift into second, push on gas pedal—look out!* We had to remember to use our turn signals, watch for other cars, look in the rear view mirror from time to time, keep an eye on the oil light—and so on.

Step by step, we continued to practice. Turn on the engine, shift, let up on the clutch, check the rear view mirror, etc. Then, in a few days (or weeks), we were jumping in, starting the car, and shooting out of the driveway without even *thinking* of the individual actions we had to concentrate so hard on when we first started. We could finally drive because we had learned to isolate each principle and practice each one (making many mistakes in the process). We could do the whole because we learned the parts.

So it is with writing. You must learn to isolate the elements of fiction. First you learn what the individual elements are—then you isolate one and work at it until you can do it well. Then you zero in on another until it is mastered.

"But—what about the rest of the elements while I'm concentrating on one?"

The rest will suffer of course. What did you expect?

Actually there are only three basic elements of fiction: plot, character, and setting (the matter of style is important, but would require another book), but I have broken each of these into subdivisions.

The story line moves on all three—plot, setting, character. Plotting must be done *before* you begin to write. Some experienced writers have learned to create as they go, but I wouldn't advise a beginner to try this method. In the section on plot, you will learn how to move from the simple plot idea to the final chapter outline. But plot is not just a series of "This happened—then this happened—then that happened." The plot of any work of fiction is based on *change*, but these changes are usually due to something in the external *setting* (such as a drought or a war) or a change in the internal *character* (such as sickness or good fortune) which makes the person different.

Once the plot is roughly in place (and it is always subject to change, for sometimes a character takes over and demands more space), you can concentrate on the other elements—dialogue, for example. Study the dos and don'ts, then go back and fix up the mess. Then move to the setting and do the same.

The day will come when you can sit down and write a piece of fiction that has an exciting plot, a setting that moves the action along, characters that are alive and well, dialogue that sparkles, vivid imagery, a variety of sentence lengths and types, and lots of other good stuff. And you'll do it all with infinitely more ease than when you first started.

Not every time, of course. Even Homer nodded—and I suspect that Shakespeare had writer's block from time to time. But the expert so masters the individual skills that he makes the whole thing look simple.

That's why he's an expert. Master the parts and the whole will be right.

My approach to writing the novel focuses on individual skills. I suggest that you get a ringed notebook, for you will be adding to and throwing away constantly.

The order of the book is simple. The first part deals with plot, the second with character development, the third with setting and the fourth with marketing and a few other matters.

One final note as you start on your novel writing adventure: You must take lots of practice shots. Basketball players invest hour upon hour to eventually dunk balls that really count; likewise, writers "waste" a lot of time writing words that "don't count." *But they do count.* I have several long manuscripts in my closet that will never see publication. But I learned many things in the act of writing them that I could learn no other way. They are my "practice shots," and I don't regret them.

Remember the story about the man who approached the hippie and asked, "How do I get to Carnegie Hall?"

I give you the same advice the hippie gave the gentleman: "Practice, man! Practice!"

Writers indulge in two basic activities:

1. Writing—they take practice shots.

2. Reading—they read the best of the kind of writing they want to do. If you want to write western novels, read the works of Ernest Haycox or Luke Short. They do it right and you will gain much by osmosis.

We'll talk more about how to use the writings of others later in this book. What's important is to get *you* started writing. Let's go.

∽

Plot Construction

Boy gets girl. Boy loses girl. Boy gets girl.

This old Hollywood cliché embodies the essence of plot—conflict. In this chapter you will learn how to build the framework of a novel. I have stripped away all ornamentation, leaving only the bare bones. The framework consists of six steps, and for each step you will use a form. You may be tempted to skip one of the steps, but I urge you to master this; later you will find ways to take shortcuts or to elaborate on the process. The six steps are as follows:

I.   State your *genre* in a single word or phrase.
II. State your *theme* as simply as possible.
III. State your plot in a *single sentence*.
IV. Divide your plot into *sections*.
V.   Create single sentence *chapter headings*.
VI. Fill out chapter headings into *paragraph summaries*.

What you will have is a pyramid with the smallest unit on top (the subject) and a broad base (chapter material) on the bottom.

Now let's take these plot elements one at a time.

I. State Your *Genre* in a Single Word or Phrase

It took me a long time to discover that the word *genre* is just a fancy word for "kind of." What *kind of* novel do you want to write? This may sound simplistic, but I am amazed at how many inexperienced writers try to create a long piece of fiction without a clear idea of their basic goal. Detective story? Western? Romance? Is it long or short? Serious or humorous? Does it have a message or is it pure escapism? Or none of the above?

Each of these genres requires a unique approach. A western novel has little in common with a regency romance. The two require different mindsets on the part of the writer and different styles of prose.

Imagine the cover of the kind of a novel you long to see your name emblazoned on. Identify this specific category and write it down. Christian detective novel. Regency romance. Fictional biography. Political satire. War novel. Whatever. The act of writing this down will help you focus on the requirements of the genre you've chosen.

Once you've chosen your genre, read a thousand books of that kind. That's the way you begin to understand what's required of you in your genre.

II. State Your *Theme* as Simply as Possible

What do I mean by *theme?* Basically, the theme of a piece of fiction reflects the *central idea* of the work, and in most cases the author's *values*. For example, the theme of Charles Dickens' novel *Bleak House* is "judicial systems are terribly corrupt and unfair." This is not the plot. The story's setting could just as easily be Russia as England. Tolstoy used the same theme of perverted judicial systems in his books set in Russia and American writers have done the same, as in *Cool Hand Luke*.

The theme of a book usually deals with a universal problem—

one that has occurred in all civilizations, ancient and contemporary. Let me use an old piece of literature to illustrate this.

Are you interested in ancient Greek burial rites? Probably not. Neither am I, but I have admired a certain play named *Antigone* by Sophocles for many years.

The plot is simple. A young Greek girl's brother is killed in battle and the king forbids burial for him. The Greeks believed that those who were not buried with certain rites were doomed to eternal woe. Antigone, the youthful sister of the slain warrior, chooses to disobey the king. She buries her brother, knowing that she will be executed for doing so—and is, in fact, put to death.

That's the *plot*. But the *theme* is "Shall an individual do the right thing and suffer for it—or shall he give in to the forces that pressure him to do the wrong thing and escape the penalty?"

This problem is not just a Greek one. The details may change, but men and women and young people from all times and cultures are forced to make this choice.

John Grisham's protagonist in his best-selling *The Client* runs into this internal conflict when he must choose between the Mafia and honor, as does Huckleberry Finn when forced to choose whether to turn in Jim, the runaway slave (as the law demands), or refuse because he loves Jim.

The fact that you are reading this book is evidence that you are interested in values, in matters of right and wrong—how to write a *Christian* novel. The Christian novel differs from the secular novel insofar as values are concerned. For example, Jack London was a naturalistic writer who believed (and dramatized in his books) that life had no meaning. Christian novelists, such as Jeanette Oke, believe that life does have meaning and her books proclaim this viewpoint. But writing technique does not change no matter what the moral stance of the writer may be. Both Jack London and Jeanette Oke must follow the principles of good writing or produce a poor work. It is true that some novels (such as those of Jack London) reflect a moral viewpoint which I abhor—but are "good" novels from the standpoint of technique. By the same token, some "Christian" novels are so poorly done that no matter how much I agree with the basic philosophy, I can hardly read them!

The fictional techniques used to develop novels with Christian values and those with worldly values are the same. Character, plot, and setting are developed the same way in each. The difference is in the theme. Your work as a writer of Christian fiction will reflect biblical principles.

But on *which* biblical principles will you focus? Which Christian theme? That is your choice. In my novel *The Dixie Widow* I chose the theme of *unforgiveness*. Many nonfiction writers have tried to handle this theme through psychology and other social methodology, but I am convinced that only the biblical principle works. "For if you forgive men when they sin against you, your heavenly Father will also forgive you. But if you do not forgive men their sins, your Father will not forgive your sins" (Mt 6:14-15), the Scriptures plainly state. "If you will not forgive others," God says, "I will not forgive you." My novel stresses that bitterness against others must be repented of before anyone can know peace.

So, you want to write a novel with Christian values, but which ones? You can't deal with them *all* in one book and that is where choosing your *theme* is a matter of vital importance.

I suggest you make a list of problems that we face:

1. Hypocrisy in the church
2. Fallen spiritual leaders
3. Loss of faith among God's people
4. Attacks by the enemy on the church
5. Christian women who have lost husbands (or vice versa)

How long a list is possible? Will there ever be a time free of conflict as we go about living out the life of Jesus Christ in this world? Your list will be endless.

You can read many novels today which communicate false themes, such as the themes set forth by Hemingway—"Enjoy life on earth, because there's nothing else."

Christians know better and it is our privilege and our duty as

Christian writers of fiction to write powerful stories which set forth a more excellent way.

III. State Your Plot in a *Single Sentence*

This is often difficult, but only because the writer has not sifted through enough chaff to get to the grain. It is the book stripped to the stark skeleton. Nobody loves a skeleton, but it's what keeps us from being jellyfish.

Boil down a novel you know well to a single sentence. If you were to choose *The Red Badge of Courage*, for example, you would arrive at something like: "A young Union soldier who is unsure of his own courage runs away in battle, but later proves his mettle under fire." That is not the novel, of course, but isn't that the heart of it? Even complex plots, such as Dickens' *Bleak House* with all of its mazelike twists and turns, can be reduced to a single statement: "The evils of the legal processes destroy a young man." What about *Gone with the Wind*? Isn't it really a quite simple story?

What you are doing when you read a book and pluck out the parts is *analysis*. What you are doing when you create your own plot is *synthesis*. Studying what professional writers have done with plot is a helpful exercise. Because I know it better than any other, I have used my own work to show you how a novel must grow from a subject to a fully developed plot.

My series of novels based on American history, *The House of Winslow* (Bethany House Publishers), consists of a number of novels approximately three hundred pages long, each dealing with a member of the Winslow family living in a critical period of history.

Since a series begins with book one, I chose the obvious for the first one: a novel dealing with the *Mayflower* and the pilgrim fathers. This is the subject, but a subject is not a book. I needed a basic theme concept. As I attempted to find this element, the idea crossed my mind, "Why not have one of the passengers on the *Mayflower* not in sympathy with the idea of going to the New World for noble reasons?" This brainstorm brought in an element called *conflict*, an essential part of all fiction.

The idea crossed my mind. That's the sort of sentence that is somewhat maddening. *How do I get ideas about plot to cross my mind?* is what most of us ask. There is no easy answer to this question. I can give you the mechanics of plotting, but you must come up with your own ideas. Ideas come in their own time; you must *wait* for them (be sure you jot them down). When they do come, the good ones come mixed with the bad ones. You will invest a good deal of time sorting the wheat from the chaff.

I was aware that the Crown was opposed to the pilgrims, and did all it could to drive them out of the country or imprison many of them. I put this idea into a single sentence:

> *A young man agrees to become a spy for the Crown in order to betray the pilgrims, but in the process falls in love with one of the young women and must choose between her and his loyalty to the King.*

I included several sub-plots within the structure that grew out of the original basic plot concept. I realized I would have to do much research: How big was the *Mayflower?* What did they eat on board? What was the captain's name? But these things are not *plot*—at least, not the basic plot. They are setting, which I would focus on at a later time.

The next step is difficult for some people. Some of us can cut wholes up into parts very easily, and others find it difficult. What you must do is:

IV. Divide Your Plot into *Sections*

Imagine a juicy apple pie. You can't eat the whole thing in one bite, so what do you do? You divide your pie into sections. Because you cannot handle wholes—only parts.

Simple, isn't it? And isn't it true of most work that you do? When you're about to clean a house, don't you organize the *whole* into *parts?* Part one: Dusting. Part two: Bedmaking. Part three: Vacuuming.

Why?

Once again, you can't do all of these at once, so you isolate the parts and work on them one at a time. What you must do is take your single sentence plot and cut it into slices—three or four sections.

Let's analyze. What are the sections of *The Red Badge of Courage?*

Part one: Before the battle.
Part two: In the battle.
Part three: After the battle.

What about *Great Expectations?*

Part one: Pip's childhood.
Part two: Pip's great expectations arrive.
Part three: Pip's great expectations fail.

The saga of the *Mayflower* took place in three acts based on geography. As I thought of the action for *The Honorable Imposter,* it seemed logical to break the action up into three parts:

Part one: England—before the voyage
Part two: *The Mayflower*—the voyage to America
Part three: The New World—after the voyage

What I look for is a *principle of division.* Can the action be broken up by *time?* This is the most obvious method and the best in many ways.

What about geography? Does the plot move from one location to another (as in *The Honorable Imposter*)?

Perhaps you can use multiple points of view to divide the action, as in Faulkner's *The Sound and the Fury.* In this complex novel, each of the four sections is a record of what one of the characters experienced.

You will not always be able to stick with your original plan. A character will "take over" and demand more space—as Falstaff did in Shakespeare's *Henry IV*. Or you may hit on a better principle of division. Or you may just discover that the original won't work.

If this happens, don't panic. You've hit a yellow caution light; you'll have to reorganize a bit.

V. Create Single Sentence *Chapter Headings*

Someone asked Mozart, "How do you write symphonies?"
"I don't know," he answered.
"But didn't you write them when you were eight years old?"
"Yes, but I didn't ask anyone how to do it."

It is at this stage that an instructor can only teach you the rules. This is the razor's edge that marks the difference between those who write and those who would like to write.

Follow these two steps:

A. Write out at length what you want to happen in the first section. Then boil it down to a reasonable plan.

B. Divide the action into episodes. You have to devise a way to get your characters from "here" to "there" in the section. Work out the "steps" or major incidents they must pass through to get from place to place. Let me demonstrate with the first section of *The Honorable Imposter*. Here is my rambling first attempt to develop the action in part one:

Gilbert Winslow's family forces him to become a candidate for the ministry. He is not really a religious man, and rebels against it but has no other choice. What he really loves are fast horses, beautiful women, fencing, and living like the devil.

He goes to a ball where he meets a beautiful aristocrat. He also meets her father, Lord North. North is charged by the Crown to drive the Puritans out of the country, but they are hard to find. Some of them have fled to Holland. North is impressed by Gilbert and offers him a position. It is a golden opportunity and the young man jumps at it, not the least because of his attraction to Cecily North. He is not particularly excited about the job North gives him to infiltrate the Holland group and deliver up the leaders to the Crown. But he agrees. He is opposed by a nobleman who is in love with Cecily, a powerful man who will give Gilbert much grief.

Gilbert goes to Holland and tries to gain access to the group. His own brother, Edward, is a part of it, even a leader, but he has been at odds with him for years, so he cannot use him. He meets a young woman, Humility Cooper, and decides to use her to get inside the group. She is an innocent young woman and he succeeds in making her fall in love with him.

He gets information, then goes back to England where he reports to the Crown and carries on his romance with Cecily. He also makes a firm enemy out of Lord Roth. He is ordered to return and find an opportunity to betray the leaders as soon as possible.

He returns to Holland where the *Mayflower* is due to sail. Winslow is sent to England with Humility, to alert those members of the church who are in hiding. He agonizes over the decision, and when the moment comes, finds that he cannot do it. But Lord Roth appears and reveals to Humility that the man she loves has used her, that he's a spy. He announces that he intends to turn Winslow over to the Crown on charges of treason. Gilbert determines that the pilgrims will not be arrested, and in a terrible fight, kills Roth. He is wounded in the duel, and when he comes to, finds himself on board the *Mayflower* bound for the New World. Humility hates him for his betrayal, but the pilgrims cannot leave him to be executed for killing Roth.

This section ends with Gilbert Winslow on board, hating God, and despised by most of the company for being an imposter and a traitor.

I had to break down all of the above into ten or twelve chapters. The final chapter headings went like this:

Chapter one: Lord North needs a spy.

Chapter two: Gilbert Winslow appears, romance begins.

Chapter three: Lord Roth and Gilbert fight over Cecily.

Chapter four: Gilbert goes to Holland, meets pilgrims.

Chapter five: He decides to make love to Humility to get "inside."

Chapter six: He works his way into the confidence of the leaders by becoming engaged to Humility.

Chapter seven: Winslow goes back to England to give a report, and to romance Cecily.

Chapter eight: Gilbert meets the king and is promised a rich reward if he can deliver the leaders of the pilgrims.

Chapter nine: He goes back to Holland and soon is sent with Humility to England to take the leaders to the *Mayflower* which is ready to sail.

Chapter ten: Gilbert finds he can't betray the leaders, and kills Roth to save them.

Chapter eleven: Humility hates Gilbert for using her but can't leave him to die. He wakes up on board the *Mayflower* headed for the New World.

At this stage, the work is really done. You'll need to work out dates and other matters, but once the action is "set" for the chapter, you are ready to move into the final step.

VI. Fill Out Chapter Headings into *Paragraph Summaries*

This is the fine print which enables you to fit the action into the space reserved for it. Chapter one gets the action underway. The first chapter of a novel is usually the most challenging for me. The reader knows nothing about any of my characters. I can't tell him who all of these people are; I must show him. Can I bring a character onstage who stands before the reader and says, "I am an evil man"? Of course not.

How does the reader learn that he is evil, then? By what he *does* and what he *says* and *what others say about him.* We'll study more about this when we get to the creation of character.

So in the first chapter the reader watches the people who are on stage. As they speak and act, he begins to learn a little about the conflicts in the story (for all story is conflict).

Here are the paragraph summaries I used for each chapter in *The Honorable Imposter:*

Chapter One. Lord North and his daughter, Cecily, are on their way to a ball at Simon Roth's home. Cecily is bored, thinking that it's all another attempt to marry her off. Her mother wants her to marry for money, her father wants her to marry a man who will be able to carry on his affairs. As they talk, it becomes clear that Cecily is proud and headstrong. Her father mentions that a distant relative of his, a clergyman, will be at the ball. Cecily decides in advance to snub him. They arrive at Roth's home, and he greets them. He is a cold man, but wealthy, with enough money to satisfy Lady North. She urges Cecily to stop fooling around and marry Roth.

Chapter Two. A handsome man is the sensation of the ball, the target of all the ladies. Cecily sets out to humble him and finds herself bested. He is the clergyman that her father mentioned, but she's never seen one so dashing. Her pride is bruised, but she is drawn to his good looks.

Chapter Three. Lord Roth and Winslow engage in a fencing match, and Roth is enraged when he is beaten. Lord North asks Gilbert to become a spy, to ferret out the leaders of a group that has gone underground—the puritan faction. Gilbert dislikes the idea of becoming a spy but will do anything to get out of being a clergyman. Not only will he be rich, if he succeeds, but there is Cecily.

Chapter Four. A lawyer in the pay of Lord North takes Gilbert to Holland. He goes to the house of his brother, who is a member of the group. He has to find some way to get inside the group.

Chapter Five. Gilbert attends church where he meets Bradford and others of the fellowship. He is impressed with the apparent honesty and piety of the Christians, but determined to find the hidden leaders. He meets Humility Cooper, and when he discovers that she knows these leaders, he decides to make love to her, gain her heart, then betray the group.

Chapter Six. Gilbert courts Humility. He goes to meetings and is finally accepted into the inner circle though he doesn't know where the leadership in England is hidden.

Chapter Seven. Gilbert is asked to return to England, where he reports to Lord North. He also romances Cecily. He spends much time going to balls with her, which enrages Roth. An attempt is made on his life, which he suspects to be the hand of Roth.

Chapter Eight. Gilbert goes back to Holland. It is almost time for the *Mayflower* to sail. Someone must go to England to take the hidden leaders to the ship. Gilbert and Humility are chosen, and they leave at once.

Chapter Nine. This chapter brings Gilbert face-to-face with his shameful treatment of Humility. She talks about how much she loves him, and he is forced to respond. She has never loved a man, and he knows how rotten he is. He almost tells her the truth, for he is having strong feelings for her.

Chapter Ten. They arrive at the place where the leader is concealed, but Gilbert cannot go through with the betrayal. He is about to confess, when suddenly Roth, who has followed them, shows up. He unmasks Gilbert, and Humility is horrified. Roth intends to deliver up Gilbert as well, but Gilbert fights him for the freedom of the pilgrims. Roth is killed, and Gilbert terribly wounded.

Chapter Eleven. Winslow wakes up on board the *Mayflower*. He discovers that Humility, though she despises him, would not leave him to die. He is bitter, hating God. The pilgrims distrust him and he will be forced to make the voyage and spend at least a year with the people who have much reason to despise him. He is filled with despair.

This is Part One, and the others are developed in the same manner.

I close this unit with a reminder. Plot, character, and setting may be pulled out of a work of fiction and each examined as a single element (as I have done with the plot of *The Honorable Imposter*), but each of these elements must be joined to the other before a book has life. A coroner can cut out a heart, a brain, or lungs and analyze them, but the person's life is gone.

Plot is character. Characters, growing, loving, hating, falling down, getting sick, sinning. As they *do* these things, the reader moves with the flow. That flow is the plot.

"This happened—and then this happened—and then this happened." This is *bad* plotting!

"He did *this*—and when he did, she was forced to do *that*—which meant that they had to do *that*."

As well, the story's setting cannot be isolated from its plot and its characters. It is only when all three of these work together that a book comes alive.

Learn the fundamentals—the six steps of plotting. It is the framework that ties the other elements of the story together.

Exercises – Unit One

∿ Exercise 1 ∿
State your *genre* (subject) in a single word or phrase.

A. Choose five well-known novels and classify them according to *subject*. For example, what is the subject of *The Grapes of Wrath* or of *Forty Thousand Leagues under the Sea*?

Example: *The Scarlet Letter*—historical novel
B. Create five one-sentence plots *of your own* and classify each of them.
Example: "A young boy, whose father goes to jail, has to cope with the problems this causes."—adolescent problem novel

∼ Exercise 2 ∼
State your *theme* as simply as possible.

Example: *The Scarlet Letter*—the problem of guilt

∼ Exercise 3 ∼
State your plot in a *single sentence*.

A. Choose five books you know well (preferably well-known novels), and compress the plot into a single sentence.
Example: *Huckleberry Finn* is the story of a fourteen-year-old white boy who tries to help a runaway slave escape to freedom in the pre-Civil War days.
B. Create five plots and express each in a single sentence. Show some creativity. Do not write five western plots, for example. Resist taking a shortcut here, for you will choose one of your sentence plots to use as the basis for the next exercise.
Example: *Ride the Wild River*—a western novel. When Julie Wade, age seventeen, is forced to flee from her abusive stepfather, she disguises herself as a young man, joins a wagon train bound for Oregon, and in addition to the dangers of the trail, falls in love with the scout, Jim Reno.

∼ Exercise 4 ∼
Divide your plot into *sections*.

A. Using *time* as a principle of division (if possible), divide one of the plots you created from Exercise 2 into sections.
B. Using *geography* (if possible), divide the same plot.

C. Try to create a plot division using at least one other principle of division.
Example: *Ride the Wild River* (divided by *geography*)
Part One: Fort Smith, Arkansas (Julie forced to run away)
Part Two: From Independence to the Rockies
Part Three: From the Rockies to Oregon
Part Four: Oregon City

⁓ Exercise 5 ⁓
Create single sentence *chapter headings*.

Until now you have dealt with large segments, but now you must focus on what actually takes place in the small units.

A. Using a simple book you know well, break the plot down into chapter headings. Write a brief statement of what happens in each chapter.
B. Using one of the plots you created in Exercise 4, make out complete chapter headings.
Example—See chapter headings for *The Honorable Imposter* in text.

⁓ Exercise 6 ⁓
Fill out chapter heading for one chapter into *paragraph summaries*.

Scene–the Heart of Fiction

You have completed the steps in unit one, and a plot lies before you, chapter outlines all in place. With a burst of confidence, you sit down at your word processor ready to write your very own novel, the one you've dreamed about writing—and suddenly you freeze up.

What has happened?

You have stumbled over a Mount Everest for writers, the problem of exactly *how to move the plot forward.*

"But I *know* what I want to do in this chapter!" you protest. "I want to get the hero and the heroine into the first stages of love, and I want the villain to raise his ugly head for the first time."

Fine, but you still have a number of decisions ahead of you: Do you use scene or exposition for the first half of a page? Even if you decide *scene*, you will have to ask that same question for the second half of the page. And again and again until the book (not the page or the chapter) is finished.

Exposition or Scene?

Another way to ask the above question is: Do you show or tell? You have probably heard the expression, "Show—don't tell." However, one can't show everything. If your character spends six months in jail, for example, you can't show all of that; if you did it would be incredibly dull. So you tell. "After six months in jail, Dave had lost much of his hostility."

It makes all the difference when you do what. When you use scene and when you use exposition. When you show and when you tell. Choosing the wrong mode will most certainly weaken your story line; choosing the right mode will cause your plot to unfold smoothly.

What is scene? What is exposition?

Read the two samples below carefully:

Number One

From the moment of the first shot fired at Concord, the British and the Americans fought with fierce intensity. The highly trained British solders and the farmers of the countryside met in several pitched battles, and these affairs were usually bloody and fierce.

Number Two

Slowly, inexorably, the grenadiers and the Royal Marines came on. A voice said, "No firing—hold your fire!" Laddie's finger was on the trigger, and there was a taste of fear in her mouth—but it was fear of killing rather than of being killed. She could see their faces clearly now—some of them fat and some thin; some sunburned and some pale, and the white of nervous eyes were in all the faces.

"Fire!" came a sudden command, and a ragged sheet of flame belched out from the hundreds of rifles and muskets in the hands of the Americans. As the smoke cleared, Laddie saw that entire ranks were down, men thrashing and screaming, while their comrades stepped over them. She heard balls whistling over her head, and ten feet to her right a man suddenly stood up, shot in the throat. He was trying to speak but only spewed out a ragged stream of bright scarlet blood, fell down, kicked the ground and died.

Men were dropping all along the line, but the toll on the charging Redcoats was terrible. The hill was covered with bodies—some still, and some feebly trying to crawl away, many writhing like cutworms. Time seemed to stand still, and Nathan could not remember a time other than this. He seemed to have been on the hill firing and taking aim forever, and it came as a shock when he heard Laddie crying out, "Nathan! They're leaving!"

What's the difference between number one and number two? Number One is *exposition*; it *tells* you that something happened. Number Two is *scene*; it *shows* you something happening.

This unit will deal with the use of *scene* only. Unit three will take up summary and other devices for moving the plot forward.

When do you use scene? Basically you *show* (scene) for three reasons.

I.   To Reveal Character
II. To Dramatize Theme
III. To Create Texture

Study these carefully; they are your most potent tools.

I. To Reveal Character

When you state a fact, you convey information, you *tell* the reader something. For example, the following sentence tells the reader something about James Bunden:
"James Bunden was a cruel man."

No one could mistake the *meaning* of that sentence. But put that same information into a scene, and you show the reader something about James Bunden:

As Bunden hurried down the street, a pitiful cripple on crutches moved in front of him holding out a cup. Bunden never slowed his pace, but with one sweeping blow drove the helpless cripple sprawling on the sidewalk. The cup clattered along the pavement, the few pennies rolled away, but Bunden never gave the man a single glance or a second thought.

What a difference. The telling of Bunden's character is smooth, and the reader slips right over it. But the dramatizing of the same material scrapes against the reader's mind *and* heart.

In *The Honorable Imposter*, the hero, Gilbert Winslow, is a ladies' man. I could have quite simply *told* the reader this facet of his character. But since this part of his personality played a critical part in the novel, I needed to do more than tell the reader about it; I created a scene that would carry this message about him. The scene does double duty, for it gives the first look at Lady Cecily North. I quote at length from the novel. The scene takes place at an aristocratic ball, and the reader has just learned that Lady Cecily is bored with her suitors:

"The crop of men isn't much tonight, I'm afraid—except for *him*, of course."

Cecily followed the direction of Mary's gaze and saw a man dressed in a uniform which bespoke the military, but which she could not recognize. "Who is he? I haven't seen him before," she said.

"He came in about thirty minutes ago," Mary whispered. "He's been watching all the ladies ever since. I think he's trying to decide which one to honor with his presence. My! Look how tall he is! And that hair!"

"Probably cross-eyed and gap-toothed behind that mask," Cecily shrugged.

"Look, Cecily! He's coming this way! I think he's chosen *you!* Do you feel honored?"

"I feel he's an insolent puppy who needs to be brought to heel." Cecily smiled slowly behind her fan. "It's a task I delight in."

"I don't know, Cecily," Mary whispered quickly. "He doesn't look like a puppy."

"Watch!" Cecily hissed. "We'll teach him to beg."

"Lady, will you take pity on a poor stranger? I will be lost forever if you refuse to dance with me!"

The voice was low and husky, and the eyes that peered behind the mask were the bluest she'd ever seen—blue as a cornflower. There was a humorous light in them that mocked at the humility of the words, for there was nothing humble in his figure. Tall and lean, like the rapier he wore at his side, there was an athletic smoothness to his bow as there had been to his walk. The mask he wore was thin, not concealing the wedge-shaped face that began with a broad bronze brow and tapered down to a jutting chin bearing a small white scar. The scar drew attention to his wide mouth; a crooked smile exposed perfect even teeth that gleamed in the light of the fires.

Cecily took in the square, well-shaped hands, the strong wrists and shapely arms, the legs set off by the tight fitting doublet and hose, then said languidly, "A lost soul? Then you must find a priest. There is one over there—Bishop Laud. I'm sure he will help you to find your way."

"Ah, Lady, the bishop can only save a soul; it is not my soul that is lost but my heart."

"Indeed? Then you need a surgeon. I recommend Mr. Devereaux. He knows all about hearts and their problems."

The wide mouth turned upward in a quick smile, and the blue eyes sparkled gaily as he said, "Not so, fair Lady. He would find nothing wrong with my heart, could he take it out and examine it. For it is not what is in my heart that brings me to death, but what is not there—your lovely self, Lady."

It was the language of courtly love, usually innocent enough. Cecily had seen a performance of *Romeo and Juliet*, and the word play between the two young lovers was light, clever, and often stinging. She was quick-witted enough to play the game well, and as for the young man who stood before her, she realized his wit was as keen as his eyes were bright. For the first time in her life she had found a man who could match her wit; indeed, sometimes his words flowed so smoothly she found herself trapped in some of the cunning conceits he laid for her.

The ease with which he led her through the dance made the exercise so natural that their conversation—filled with barbed jests and clever innuendoes—was not at all impeded.

The scene concludes with a passionate kiss which is interrupted by Lord Roth, jealous suitor for Cecily's hand. This in turn leads to a duel which reveals Gilbert Winslow's skill with a sword—an important factor in the novel.

Now, what does the reader learn about Gilbert Winslow by reading this scene?

1. He is handsome.
2. He is tall and athletic.
3. He can put the moves on an attractive woman.
4. He is quick-witted.

And what do we learn about Lady Cecily North?

1. She is very proud.
2. She is highly educated in literature.
3. She is witty.

It would be so simple to offer all of this information to the reader in one sentence: "Gilbert Winslow was a tall, handsome man, quick-witted with smooth manners—and he loved to use all of his assets for the purpose of charming pretty women."

But in this case, can that one sentence effectively accomplish what scene can?

For years I've told my writing students, "I don't believe anything anyone *tells* me; I believe what I *see.*"

That is not rhetoric. America did not declare war on Germany in 1917 because they read, "German soldiers are committing atrocities in Belgium." No, it was not until we *saw* the pictures of the atrocities that we moved toward war.

Notice how the scene above reveals character by the basic methods:

1. What a character says
2. What a character does
3. What others say about him

The entire plot revolves around one idea: *Gilbert Winslow*

makes Humility Cooper, a member of the pilgrim group, fall in love with him, then betrays that group to the civil authorities.

Only a handsome, quick-witted man with much experience with women could achieve this. I designed the above scene to set such a man before the reader.

Let's look at one more example of how a single scene can bring the character to the reader with a razor sharpness.

The title of the novel, *The Honorable Imposter*, is, of course, an oxymoron—two terms that conflict with one another. An imposter cannot be honorable, can he? If a man is honorable, he cannot be an imposter, or can he? This is the novel's basic conflict. Gilbert Winslow wants the good things of life. They lie within his grasp—if he is willing to become a spy and betray a group of good people.

By the end of chapter nine, he has fought this battle within himself, and decided to go through with the scheme. I wrote one short scene to close the chapter. Gilbert and Lucas Tiddle, a worldly lawyer, are in a carriage. Gilbert has just agreed to become a spy. In this brief scene he struggles with the moral problem—and Tiddle is no help!

"I'll go with you to the ship, my boy," Tiddle said at once. "Get our things and I'll engage a carriage."

They left shortly, Tiddle going over the detailed aspects of business that Gilbert would need to attend to in Holland.

"Your mind isn't on business, is it, Gilbert?" Tiddle asked suddenly. "I see you're still not easy in your mind—on this business of turning Brewster in."

"It's different from the duel in Dead Man's Lane," Gilbert said vehemently. "I'll lose no sleep over that one! But if William Brewster is like the others, he's no criminal!"

"He is in the eyes of the King."

"Then the King is wrong!"

"Hush, man!" Tiddle said with a glance upward toward the driver. "D'ye not know men have gone to the Tower for saying less?"

Gilbert shrugged, then forced a smile. "I know you're a

lawyer, Lucas, and accustomed to putting moral questions in neat little boxes. Well, I can't do that! To me Brewster is a human being—from what I hear, a fine one! I can't hand him over to torture and death because he printed a sermon that offended the King!"

Sadly Tiddle shook his head. "I fear it's like that. The world's a bad place for romantics and idealists, Gilbert. As I once told you, you must pack your sense of honor away, retaining only the name, and join the rest of us who are busily selling our souls to the devil."

"This world or the next, eh, Lucas?" Gilbert sighed. Then he turned to face the lawyer. "Let me ask you, are you a Christian?"

"I am a member of the Established Church, Gilbert," Tiddle said evenly. "I pay my tithes, take communion when I am obliged to by the bishop, and do not give aid to dissenters. This is my religion. Having done those things, it is up to the Church of England to keep me out of hell!"

The coach rattled along, and Gilbert watched a high-flying falcon stoop to take a field sparrow in an explosion of feathers. Finally he said heavily, "The world would be a much simpler place—if it weren't for God and all that."

"No doubt—but it's the only world we have, Lad," Tiddle echoed sadly.

I remember only faintly the writing I have done in the past. However, I remember clearly how hard I worked on this brief scene. In my first draft, I tried to take a short cut. Just have Gilbert betray Brewster and be done with it. I tried to *tell* of this in exposition, rather than *show* it in scene, and it ended up full of windy, preachy statements. I needed to position Gilbert's inner struggle clearly before the reader. For without a struggle, the plot would fall apart.

A scene must do more than shuffle the characters through a few pages so that you are nearer the end and the royalty check. Each scene must carry weight, a great deal of weight.

II. To Dramatize Theme

Most of us suffer the temptation to just tell the facts. But literature is not "telling the facts." The theme of *The Scarlet Letter* could be stated as follows: "Individuals should not conceal their wrongdoing, for it will surface and destroy them."

True enough, but that is *not* Hawthorne's novel. All respectable works of fiction do more than state the expositional facts about a theme. These novels present consecutive scenes of action that bear within themselves the unspoken essence of the book's theme.

The Honorable Imposter is about the pilgrim fathers who believed so strongly in God that they risked everything they had to be faithful to what they felt were his commands.

My problem was to convey the sense of this kind of faith. I set several scenes in church and used some sermon excerpts. But I wanted more than that. (I *always* want more than that—and so should you.) I wanted to show a dramatic demonstration of this faith. I put this scene in a chapter that I designed for the purpose of showing the reader that the faith of Bradford and the others was not just a theological position. This chapter is entitled "The Storm." It is historically accurate; such a storm did take place. Much of the material came from Bradford's own journal.

The storm that struck on the morning of September 17 was like nothing Captain Jones had ever seen. Coming out on deck, he stopped dead still, so suddenly that Sam Fuller rammed into him. "Look at that!" he breathed in a small whisper.

"What is it?" Brewster asked.

"Storm coming—faster than I've ever seen!"

A black cloud dropped down, making a shelf across the horizon and moving so fast across the choppy waters they could trace its progress.

"All hands!" Jones shouted. "Man the sails! Batten down! Batten down!" As the crew came tumbling out of the ship, Jones said, "Get to the passengers, Brewster! This is going to be pretty rough!"

In a matter of minutes the main top sail ripped up one side and blew out in ribbons, cracking like gigantic whips.

The ship began beating back and forth before the terrible force of the headwind, like an animal running up and down. The light of day failed as the blackness of the cloud wrapped a sable blanket around the plunging ship, and the last flag of daylight, a thin streak of silver-white, was blotted out by the rolling cloud. The dull roaring rose at times to a high-pitched scream, drowning out the creaking of the timbers and the fluttering of the tattered sails.

The seamen fought their way along the tilting decks, grabbing desperately to rails, masts, lines as they tried to control the ship.

"Take in sail! In with your top sails. Lower your main sails, lower the foresail..." Jones shouted.

Stripped of all canvas, the *Mayflower* was thrown about like a ball. "Get a few feet of canvas up on the poop or she'll founder!" the captain shouted, and Coffin was nearly washed overboard as the crew rigged a small sail.

The masts swayed crazily against the dark sky, and the bow lifted over the mountainous swells, a terrific shudder shaking her as she plowed into the head of the mountain of water. She was flooded below as wave after wave broke over her.

Below deck there was bedlam. Water ran everywhere—through the hatch covers, under the two doors opening out onto the waist deck, and through many loosened seams in the main decking, trickling and seeping down from deck to deck till it reached the bilge in the bottom of the ship.

William Brewster peered through the darkness cut only by the occasional glow of a single candle through panes of an opaque lantern, thinking with the others that each roll of the ship might be the last.

Most of the women were crying as well as the children, but suddenly William Bradford's voice rang out over the screaming wind, "Lord, do not grind our people and let them be lost! Deliver us, as you delivered Jonah and Daniel!"

Then he raised his voice in a psalm, and there in the depths, the voices of others joined in:

Jehovah feedeth me, I shall not lack
In grassy folds he down doth make me lie
He gently leads me quiet waters by
He doth return my soul, for his name sake
In paths of justice leads me quietly.

But still the wind thundered and the ocean smashed at the ship; then as their quaking voices began the next verse, with a crash like a cannon shot, a main beam amidship cracked and buckled!

This scene goes on at length, dwelling on the crisis. If the main beam is not repaired, the ship will break up and crew and passengers will be lost. William Bradford says that he will pray for God to deliver them. Captain Jones, who is not a Christian man, scoffs in unbelief. The situation gets much worse, and when it seems that all is lost, Gilbert remembers a large iron jack that he has seen below. He uses it and the beam is lifted, thus saving the ship. Again, this is historically accurate. I close the scene in such a way as to underline the faith of Bradford and the pilgrims—and to show how their faith is beginning to affect Gilbert Winslow:

A cheer went up as the upright jack pressed against the beam and slowly pushed it up until it was even.

"That'll hold until calm weather," the carpenter said. "Then we'll spike a splint across that break and re-peg it to the upper deck."

Suddenly William Brewster's voice cut through the hold like a trumpet—feeble, perhaps, but reaching every ear. "The Word of the Lord has come to pass! He has sent deliverance!"

Christopher Jones was flooded with relief. The *Mayflower* was his livelihood, his love, his security. Five minutes ago, he would not have given a farthing for the chances of saving her; now it was a matter of riding out the storm.

He raised a hand that was not entirely steady to wipe the water from his face, then he turned to face Brewster who was standing knee-deep in water with his hands raised to heaven and a light of joy on his thin face.

"I think Mr. Winslow really deserves some credit," he said softly. "It was quick thinking, man, and I'm in your debt."

Gilbert stood there, staring at the jack, saying nothing, and then he felt a hand on his shoulder and looked up to see William Bradford standing beside him.

"Mr. Winslow, we're all in your debt."

Gilbert was caught off guard. Bradford had said not one good word to him since he had come aboard, and yet the honesty of the man was not to be denied. He looked at the angular planes of Bradford's face and asked impulsively, "Surely you can't think the Lord would use a sinner to do his work—with so many saints around?"

William Bradford was a strong man, but he bowed his head at that question, and there was a look of pain in his dark eyes as he looked around at the people in the hold—saints and sinners.

"I am not as certain as I once was in some things. When I was younger, I felt that it was a simple matter to identify God's children. Lately, I have wondered if I was not often hasty in my youthful judgments."

Gilbert stared at him, then said in a hard tone, "Well, there's no doubt in *my* mind about this business. I saw the jack, and when we needed it, I remembered it. Nothing of God in it."

He sounded like a man trying to convince himself, but Edward put a hand up and said quietly, "There's some of God in everything, Gilbert—as you'll know before he's finished with you!"

Yes, this scene reveals some things about the characters, but it also clearly demonstrates the faith of the pilgrims. A short cut wouldn't work. It is necessary to *show* the storm in all its fury, for it is the awful danger that serves as a foil for the faith of Bradford and the others.

I could have summarized this scene: "On September the 17th, a terrible storm struck the *Mayflower,* breaking a main deck member. The pilgrims prayed, and someone remembered an iron jack, which enabled them to save the ship."

Pretty thin stuff when contrasted with the *scene.*

III. To Create Texture

C.S. Lewis once made a critical remark about the works of a certain famous novelist. "They are no good," he said, "because they have no *weather* in them!"

Readers need a sense of the environment. This comes through as we use one or more of the five senses in our writing. Over my Mac Plus hangs a drawing of five objects—a nose, a pair of eyes, a hand, an ear, and a tongue. They are poorly drawn (the tongue looking more like a hot dog than anything else!), but they remind me that readers want to see, hear, touch, taste, and smell. And they can only do this through *concrete* images. A pile of rotting garbage, a ruby-throated hummingbird, a mouth full of quinine.

Part of my task in writing *The Honorable Imposter* was to create a sense of the hardships of the voyage. I chose to highlight the terrible tragedy of Dorothy Bradford's death at the end of the voyage of the *Mayflower.* Almost all historians agree that she lost her mind on the voyage and committed suicide by drowning. I made Dorothy a tragic figure, totally unfitted for life in the raw, which she was, according to all reports. I foreshadowed her death by letting her slowly deteriorate mentally on the voyage. She grew physically ill and suffered nightmares. She often sang a song: *I'm a little lost lamb, a little lost lamb, far, far away from home.*

I included the following scene which portrays the actual suicide. Gilbert and Humility are sitting beside the sick woman, but when Gilbert leaves and Humility drops off to sleep on the floor, Dorothy awakens.

Dorothy had slept off and on, but when she awakened and found her hand released and Humility lying on the floor asleep, she lay there for a long time staring at the candle.

The winds were whistling through the sails, and the motion of the boat was hypnotic.

"I'm a poor lost lamb—I'm a poor lost lamb... " she breathed softly, then put the cover aside and stood up. The cabin was cold, and she shivered as the air struck her. She leaned forward peering at Humility intently; then a small smile touched her lips and she put a finger on her lips and whispered, "You sleep, Mama—I'll go outside and play with my dolls."

Softly she tiptoed through the cargo hold, carefully avoiding the sleeping forms, and when she got to the ladder leading upward, she giggled with her hand over her mouth. She climbed the stairs and went out on deck.

The ocean was a beast, rolling from side to side and growling deep, but she did not heed the crashing of the waves against the sides, but made her way quickly to the bow. There she leaned out and stared down at the water that seemed to be alive.

"I'm a little lost lamb... " she murmured, and leaned forward to see into the green depths of the great water that licked the sides of the dark hull.

The prow went down sharply, and then rose high in the air, and the sudden movement frightened her. She began to cry, calling out, "Papa! Papa! Where are you, Papa?"

Her thin cries were swallowed up by the roar of the wind, and waves licked higher up on the hull. She turned to go back along the deck, then came to a large box beside the rail.

Carefully she climbed up on top of it, then turned to look over the rail, now up to her knees. The ship seemed to drop, then lurched sideways as she started to step down, and the sudden movement threw her off balance.

Her feet slipped, and she shot over the rail crying once before she reached the freezing water, *"Oh, William!"* Then she struck the hard green water; darkness enveloped her as she went down, head over heels. The icy coldness seared her lungs, and she opened her mouth to scream, but it filled with salty water. Then she slid unto utter darkness, dragged down by the claws of a powerful undercurrent.

The tide rolled her gently toward the deep sea, her skirts wafting slowly, a sea flower, her hands white fingers of coral, her hair fine streaming sea grass.

This scene is terrible. But the voyage itself was terrible. Most of the passengers would die a worse death in the winter sickness, and this death prefigures and foreshadows that time of dying.

These, then, are the three occasions when scene is most effectively employed. Scene serves other purposes, of course, but if you will master these three, your writing will take on a vivid depth that is often missing from that which employs too much summary.

Work on the exercises carefully. The next unit deals with summary and other devices we must use to move a plot forward, but try to master scene before going on to other elements.

Exercises — Unit Two

The first two exercises, 1 and 2, deal with the use of scene to *reveal character.* Exercise 3 should illustrate the use of scene to *dramatize a theme.* Exercise 4 and 5 should demonstrate how a scene can *create texture.*

~ Exercise 1 ~

Write a scene that involves two characters. One character, Ellen, is cold and callous, almost totally selfish. The other character, Fred, is basically a kindly man, whom Ellen almost destroys.

~ Exercise 2 ~

Write a scene involving a young woman and her boss. The girl, who is highly insecure, wants to please people and be accepted. She has been put down most of her life. The boss is insensitive, caught up in his own needs.

⌒ Exercise 3 ⌒

You are writing a novel about the importance of people opening up to other people—or to put it in the negative, the danger of people isolating themselves from others. Write a scene that illustrates this. If your scene is in danger of becoming too long, include some basic information in parentheses at the beginning of the scene to set the stage:

(The following scene takes place between the protagonist and a person who *wants* to be her friend. It occurs early in the novel.)

Don't be afraid to write too much—maybe three to five pages. It takes *words* to dramatize a theme.

⌒ Exercise 4 ⌒

Reread the selection from *The Honorable Imposter* in this chapter, the scene where Dorothy Bradford commits suicide. Here, I added texture when I used the sea as a symbol of the dangerous journey and to highlight the death of a small woman. Now write a dramatic scene and at the end of your writing, explain briefly what you hoped to accomplish with the scene in the way of texture.

⌒ Exercise 5 ⌒

Write a scene in which the outer world somehow reflects the inner world of the character. If your protagonist is confused and angry inside, for example, create a setting which reflects those internal feelings. Remember to appeal to taste, touch, smell, hearing, and sight.

Unit Three

〜

Exposition

Several years ago a playwright became irritated with the artificiality of drama. "It's not like real life," he complained. "What the world needs is a play that shows life *exactly* like it is!"

He proceeded to put his concept into action. He hired a theatre and a cast, advertised in the newspaper—and the show was on.

The name of the drama was—*LIFE*. The stage was an apartment, a living room, a combination dining room-kitchen, a bedroom. Doors led off to bathrooms and other bedrooms.

But this was not a stage setting. It was a *real* apartment. The plumbing worked, and the closets were real; clothes hung in them. "I'm tired of fake settings," the playwright said. "We'll have a *real* place, just like life."

The cast was composed, not of actors, but of *real* people. The dramatist hired a family to actually live in the apartment; a father, mother, an older boy and girl, and one young child of six agreed to live onstage.

"Time is too artificial in drama," the dramatist said. "Real life situations don't erupt and resolve themselves within a two-hour period." Therefore, the box office stayed open twenty-four hours a day. One could buy a ticket at three in the morning, go in and find a seat, and watch the stage. Of course, at that time, one wouldn't

43

see much. People are usually asleep at three in the morning.

If you had gone into the theatre at two in the afternoon, you would have watched an empty stage for two or three hours. While the father and mother worked, the older children were in school, and the younger child was in a day care center.

Wouldn't this be boring?

It's life, but it's not drama. And when we go to a theatre, we go to see drama, not life.

What is drama? It is life arranged in a certain way so that we are entertained. We are not interested in watching the protagonist brush his teeth, then sit down and read a newspaper for an hour. In real life, this is what he might do, but in drama we want those elements of life set before us which present the *essence* of human experience.

What does a dramatist do? From the thousand and one mundane actions that make up "real" life, he selects certain portions from real lives of individuals, and sets them before his audience.

The problem, however, is that the "meaningful" and "critical" parts of a life do not happen in sequence, but are separated by the more mundane episodes.

The purpose of exposition is to furnish the reader with the framework on which the major thematic action takes place. In *Huckleberry Finn*, for example, Mark Twain presents several highly dramatic *scenes:* the one in which Huck and Jim discover the dead man on a wrecked ship, the scene in which Huck dresses as a girl and goes to town, and the moment when Huck has to decide whether he will turn the runaway slave in and go to heaven or help him escape and go to hell. But these scenes do not occur with machine-gun rapidity. Twain creates a world of peace and quiet, the world of the river, and after each dramatic episode, the pair return to the raft and do nothing but drift and exist.

In unit one, we discussed the importance of dramatic scenes in a novel. But a danger lurks behind the page for the writer who overdoes this method.

An editor told me about a young writer he was working with on a book. She had written screenplays for motion pictures, but this was her first novel.

"The first draft was terrible!" the editor said. "It was one scene after another, with nothing to tie them together." With some instruction, the writer eventually made the jump from screenplay to novel and has become quite successful.

Movies and TV shows are not books. They work differently, and they must be written differently. A film can use fades, dissolves, wipes, and many other camera techniques to tie action scenes together, but the writer must do this with words alone. If he fails to connect his scenes with some kind of exposition, he will have a slam-bang action novel, perhaps, but not a good work of fiction.

No one has a life filled with frenzied excitement for twenty-four hours every day, seven days a week. The human spirit couldn't stand it! No, a large part of our lives is composed of those many hours when nothing much is happening. Nothing that is worth recording for all the world to note. Life goes on slowly. We get up, eat, drink, work. Does anybody want to read about this?

Even a heroic figure such as Winston Churchill has his dull moments. A little girl popped into his room one afternoon, saw Sir Winston lying in bed, and asked, "Are you the greatest man alive?"

Sir Winston glared at her and said, "Certainly! Now, pop off, will you?"

Winston Churchill lived a dramatic and exciting life, but he had to brush his teeth just like the rest of us. If I were writing a novel about him, I would certainly not record every tooth-brushing. It would bore even *him*.

So then, the dramatic scenes in a novel must be linked together. The reader must not leave one highly pitched, emotionally charged scene only to find himself thrown headlong into another one and then another.

What exposition does is allow the reader time to breathe, to think, to consider. But that is not the only function of this device, as we shall see. Let's look at the four basic methods of exposition which you should master:

I. Summary
II. Journals
III. Letters
IV. Mini-essays

I. Summary

First, the most commonly used method of exposition: summary. By definition, a summary is an abbreviated account of a longer piece of work. In fiction, it is that part of the work which compresses a long period of time into a few words.

There is an art to writing good summary. Make it perform the following two functions. Let it:

• Convey concrete and vivid details about your characters and the story events

• Do double duty. For example, you might want to show how the passage of time is working on the character's mind. Maybe you want to refer to the novel's various conflicts.

The action is laid out at the time you construct your plot, as we have learned in unit one. But it is in the actual *writing* that you must tie the action-filled scenes together—through *exposition*.

The Honorable Imposter is a book of action, but it covers a period of many months. The action begins shortly before the *Mayflower* sails and ends after the terrible first winter when the first ship arrives from England. In chapters one, two, and three the action moves rapidly. It is filled with duels, attempted murders, dress balls, audiences with the king, and other dramatic scenes. But in chapter four Gilbert must leave that world. He has agreed to join the pilgrim group at Leyden, find out where William

Brewster is hiding, and hand him over to the king. But this cannot be done in an hour's time. It is decided that he will pretend to be an agent of Lucas Tiddle on a business trip to Leyden. This involves spending much time with Tiddle, learning his business in order to convince the Leyden group that he is what he seems to be.

No reader is really interested in the details of a clerk's duties. It would slow the action down to a walk. But since some of this is important to my novel's story line, on page forty-five I cover this period of time in a single paragraph:

> Winslow had left the university with a sense of adventure rising in him. Tiddle met him at his office, and the next three days were spent learning the rudiments of the business affairs that would occupy him in Holland. They had packed and left to pick up Howland for the journey.

At that point, as they travel by carriage to the ship, a critical *scene* takes place. This scene is called a *transition*. You need to use a transition whenever you move from one section of writing to another. Characters cannot be "beamed up" as on *Star Trek*. A transition is often only one sentence, but between major sections, a small scene is necessary. I have discussed this scene fully in unit two, but notice that if I had left out the exposition of Winslow's activities at Tiddle's office, he would have abruptly stepped straight from an important love scene with Cecily right into the streets of Leyden with no warning.

At this point, Gilbert is still in London. How does he get to Leyden? The whole journey is compressed into part of one page, and it employs a device you should master. It looks like a *scene*, but it is really exposition. It goes like this:

> "There's Leyden just ahead, Gilbert." Lucas nodded out of the carriage window. He turned to look at the young man slumped in the seat beside him and gave a wink in the direction of Howland sitting across from him. "Don't tell me you're still

seasick, lad? Come now, you can't have anything in your stomach—not after the way you heaved all across the Channel!"

Gilbert raised a hollow-eyed face the color of old ivory. The voyage had been a nightmare for him, for he had discovered with the first roll of the twenty-ton merchantman that he was no sailor.

By the time the ship touched at Amsterdam, Gilbert had long ceased to be afraid that he would die—he only wished he *could!* Howland had practically carried him off the ship and put him in a carriage, and he had been unconscious for most of the trip to Leyden. They had stopped for a meal at a small inn, and while his companions had wolfed down a huge meal of veal and cheese, Gilbert had managed to keep down a half pint of cold ale and a few swallows of fresh bread. Deciding he was going to live, he finally managed to sit up and take in the scenery that unrolled as they made their way toward Leyden—mostly flat fields silvered with winter's touch. Windmills everywhere turned their huge sails, and neat stone and clapboard houses dotted the fields. "We'll put you off at your brother's house," Tiddle said. "He's expecting you. I wrote him myself."

Then follows the critical scene in which Gilbert must be reconciled with his brother or the whole game is off. The exposition is more than just a blunt statement of fact. I could have written:

Gilbert and Tiddle crossed the English Channel in order for Gilbert to meet with his brother, Edward, so that the plot could begin to work.

This would be *adequate*, but poor writing. *Exposition*, as you can see, has some elements of scene. This is what I mean by giving your summary concrete, vivid detail. It is dramatic: "There's Leyden just ahead, Gilbert." This direct speech leads into the exposition of how they crossed the channel. I use concrete detail: "a huge meal of veal and cheese." I throw in details of the countryside; flat fields silvered with winter's touch, windmills with huge sails, neat stone and clapboard houses...

This kind of exposition does not jerk the reader from one scene to the next. I have moved Gilbert from one world to another in a smooth manner that carries the reader with him.

The next chapters are devoted to Gilbert's efforts to join the pilgrims. He focuses on Humility Cooper and succeeds in making her fall in love with him. Time after time, in these chapters, it is necessary to move the action ahead several days or to a different geographical location. At one point Lucas Tiddle is leaving to return to England. He rebukes Gilbert because the young man has made no headway in joining the pilgrim group. How long has he been trying?

I chose not to use exposition to convey this information to the reader, but simply put it in a scene, in one of Tiddle's speeches: "You've been here three days and found out nothing."

This is scene, but it is also summary. It is an effective way to reveal to the reader that time has passed. *Learn to use your characters' speeches to move the plot.* Exposition is necessary, but in one sense, the less of it, the more dramatic the fiction. Remember, don't tell me—show me.

Finally at the end of part one, Gilbert discovers that he simply *cannot* betray William Brewster. He kills Lord Roth in a duel, attempts to get Humility and Brewster on board the *Mayflower*, but falls into the hold of the ship and is knocked unconscious. They have no choice but to take him to the New World with them, for if they leave him, he will hang for the murder of Roth.

I use exposition to tell how Gilbert spends his days as the slow voyage continues.

Gilbert's wounds began to knit almost at once, and three days after leaving Plymouth, he began to get sick of the sailroom. There was nothing to read but Brewster's Bible, and when the other man was absent, Gilbert was driven from sheer boredom to read the mystic visions of Ezekiel and the lists of clean and unclean food in Leviticus.

He spent long hours thinking of Cecily and of the lost

opportunities of their life together. Now that she was lost to him, she seemed more desirable than ever, and the wealth and power which had been a mere possibility as Lord North's man, in his imagination became more solid and real than ever. A dark streak of fatalism imposed itself on his spirit, and the optimism that had been a part of his character faded as the lonely days dragged on.

What does this exposition accomplish? It takes the reader along in time, of course. But does it do anything else? Does it reveal anything about Gilbert?

In this brief passage, there is a foreshadowing of the fatalism that nearly destroys him. "A dark streak of fatalism imposed itself on his spirit."

Make your summaries do double duty. Include brief lines that highlight the conflict, or show how the action works on the character's mind or spirit. Make each summary do more than mark the passage of time. You have a page limit, so use every opportunity to develop both character and conflict.

The voyage goes on and on. I handled the passage of time this way: "They were sixty-seven days out from Plymouth, ninety-seven from Southampton. Shouts of joy and tears of relief rang on the morning air as the entire company met to view their new home."

This is almost pure summary. It is an overview of the entire voyage, and the reader now knows that the ship is at its destination. Use summary often to keep your reader aware of time and place.

They are now in the New World. I use a brief exposition to give some impression of the group's activity.

By January 3, New Plymouth was beginning to take shape, but the progress was slow. Fieldstone had to be gathered for fireplace and hearth, two-inch planks had to be sawed for walls, and the joints and cracks had to be daubed with clay.

One of the most difficult and time-consuming tasks was

thatching the roofs. They were made as they had been for gen-
erations in England, but thatch was hard to come by in Plymouth. It meant miles of tramping through the meadows and
along the creek banks to gather it, with the constant possibility
of being cut off by a surprise Indian attack.

Once again, this exposition does more than just move the
action forward through time. It shows the incredible hard work
that went into the building of the settlement. Note also the concrete detail. The words "By January 3... " are didactic, but in a
historical novel like this one, such things are necessary. A lot of
readers know their history.

I do this sort of thing again later in the novel, expanding it this
time into a half-page:

None of the firstcomers who survived ever forgot the month of
February. Whatever visions of a summery Eden remained were
drowned by the rain, the sleet and the snow, and the keen
winds that whipped across the sea to scrape faces raw and cut
the lungs with a razor's edge.

No one was ever wholly dry, and the sickness claimed new
victims almost daily. There was a fever to get houses built, for
the *Mayflower* would leave any day. Indians were never seen,
but smoke signals were visible and more than once they came
to scream at the settlers in the night.

Death became such a common visitor that the first morning
thought of Fuller was, *"Who will lie dead in their beds this
morning?"*

I tried here to encompass that terrible month, by giving
enough details to convey its horror. I wanted to create a certain
feeling in the reader as well as show the passing of February.

Better to say too much than too little, so let me again pound
this into your mind: Make exposition do more than show passage
of time.

Study good novels to learn more about the use of exposition.

Actually, the better the writing, the less you will even notice scene and exposition. Why? Because the bones won't show. Just as you do not often hear the individual instruments in a symphony; you hear the *whole*.

You can show the passage of time and space in many ways; learn to utilize them all.

II. Journals

The journal or diary conveys an intimacy lacking in ordinary speech. Used sparingly, it does double duty: it can mark the passage of time as well as reveal the inner mind of the character. It can also bring your reader close to your main character if you're using a viewpoint other than first person.

I chose to use this method in *The Honorable Imposter*. Gilbert Winslow is alone on the *Mayflower*, that is, he has no friends. His life is shattered and he has grown bitter. Under such circumstances a man might put his thoughts in a journal. I quote the first entry at length:

September 7, 1620
The keeping of a journal is the business of lovesick maidens.

Yet here am I, Gilbert Winslow, sitting in the dark sail locker of the *Mayflower*, scribbling away by the light of a stubby candle, my only companion a religious fanatic.

The cabin is no darker than my own heart. How quickly life can reverse itself! Was it only a few brief hours ago I was secure in the certainty of place and fortune in the service of the most powerful lord of England, happy in the hope of a beautiful woman? And now, here I sit in this dank hole with my life wounded far worse than my leg—which by the way, throbs as if a demon were pounding a white-hot spike into it!

Brewster has gone to sleep, and I do not need to write any longer. I began writing to keep him from talking to me any more. He is so confounded *cheerful* in the face of everything!

Of course *he* is safe now, bound for his New World where he can preach to the naked savages to his heart's content. To give him his due, he is an honest man, quite convinced that this world is but a bit of practice for the world to come. They all think that, actually seeming to *enjoy* suffering! They claim hardship endured for God is like money in the bank, that it will build up compound interest until they get there to enjoy it!

But trying to talk to these fanatics about hard *fact* is like talking to a tree! They just give you a smile dripping with sweetness and ask, "Why, where's your faith, brother?"

In a few weeks, after scurvy hits and teeth start dropping out, I'd ask a few of them, "Where's *your* faith, brother?"

No, I will not. That's the bitterness of my own heart.

I have only one hope. I am strong and I will endure this voyage. I will endure the beginnings—and I will be aboard the first ship that comes to this accursed place!

One thing I will *not* do—I will not join these people in any way! Brewster is a fine man—one of the few on this earth who would forgive another for such as I planned to do to him. But he'll starve or be killed by savages like the rest. Humility—I can't write about her.

I will give these people the strength of my arm—but not one inch of ground in my heart—so help me God!

Two things happen in this journal entry. The date fixes the exact time in the reader's mind. Secondly, the reader is able to watch Gilbert's mind at work; his attitudes, fears, and hopes come through. In this case, the journal entry is an effective device. Gilbert would not *say* these things aloud to anyone, for he has no one to say them to, no friend or confidant. The flavor of his spirit comes out, his rigid determination not to become a Christian, his bitterness as he's watched his plans go down in flames, and the spirit of fatalism that has come over him.

When using a journal, make sure the character's true voice comes through, that the attitudes, words, and manner are compatible with the character. Gilbert, an educated man, is completely in character when he writes rather poetically, "The cabin is no darker than my own heart." But those words would be out of character for a practical man like Tiddle or an unlettered carpenter like John Alden. The entry is much more emotional than Gilbert would ever allow himself to reveal outwardly, and that is the value of a journal or diary.

Gilbert's attitudes in the first journal entry are intensified and augmented:

> September 17, 1620
> I am not sure of anything. I suppose a man has two sides and there will never be a world which will please both sides. One side of him is going to be hot and the other side cold. Maybe this earth is for right-handed people, the left-handed ones will cry in it!
>
> Which is my world? England seems as alien as Venus. Would I go there, get rich, marry Cecily? Why do I still look in Humility's eyes and think of New Testament verses?
>
> I guess there is God and the devil in me—maybe in everyone.
>
> What happened today in the hold? They prayed and I thought of a jack. Did the God who flung those millions of stars in space give a hang for this fragment of a ship on an insignificant journey to a savage land? Brewster says God stepped in. He claims I was given the right answer, and that may be true—but I can't believe it! Whatever God is up there has forgotten about us long ago. But how comforting it would be to believe in Brewster's God!

Can you see the *tension* in this passage? By the end of the book, Gilbert becomes a believer in Brewster's God, but he doesn't come to that position in an hour; the passage from unbelief to faith is a laborious one, and it must be so recorded if it is to be believable.

This device is artificial to a degree, but then that could be said of any method of fiction. The crucial question is how much to use it. Too much is worse than none at all, I feel. Make it count. Make it natural. Make it brief.

In my novel, I've used the ship's log to pinpoint the action and show how an objective observer views the protagonist. Since Captain Jones is a significant character in the book, the log also reveals how his mind works. The log also authenticates the novel's history.

Log: September 12.

Yesterday two stowaways were discovered. One of them, Mr. William Brewster, has been a fugitive from the King's justice for some years as a result of certain writings; the other is a young man named Gilbert Winslow. Since there is no possibility of escape, I have not placed them under arrest, but on the return to England, I will do so and turn them over to the proper authorities.

Log: September 20.

Sighted land at dusk. It appears to be Cape Cod, somewhere off the high bluffs of Truro. It being late, we will search the coast for a harbor on the morrow.

Seaman Jeffery Daggot was lost at sea after falling overboard. Attempts to recover his body were in vain. May God have mercy on his soul. [This reference was not strictly true. Winslow has killed Daggot in self-defense. But this entry shows that the captain of the ship is growing in sympathy for Gilbert.]

Log: January 14th.

Follows the order of deaths since landing: Edward Thompson, the first to die in the New World; Jasper Moore, James Chilton, Dorothy Bradford, 11th December; Richard Britteridge, 21st December; Degory Priest, 1st January; John Langemore, Christopher Martin, 8th January; Mrs. Martin the following day. Weather continues cold, with snow and ice in abundance. Crew is restless, desiring to return to England while supplies permit. My decision is to remain at least until shelter is completed for all settlers.

These entries do double duty, especially the last one, for it not only throws the cold hard light of death on the pilgrims, but it shows that the captain has joined their party, in spirit at least.

The third device you can use to glue dramatic scenes together is:

III. Letters

In the eighteenth century a style of novel appeared called "epistolary novels," which consisted only of a series of letters. The most famous of these, *Pamela,* contained a young girl's letters and was a great success in its day.

The day of the epistolary novel is gone, but the use of letters as a transitional device is still an option. Letting the audience in on a letter from one of the characters has several advantages.

It has *immediacy.* It is the character speaking directly. It is sometimes more honest than a speech. It serves the same purpose as a diary in that we all write things to our friends that we would never utter in public. The letter can become a *confessional.* The writer is saying, "I must tell you something that is so important to me, I can't tell anyone else."

Early in the action, Gilbert writes a letter to Lucas Tiddle. He has just agreed to become an imposter, and the tenor of the letter is cheerful (as it will not be later on). It reveals that at this point he is rather a rogue—especially when it comes to using women for his own purposes:

My dear Tiddle,
You left me under a cloud, suggesting that I would be rather useless so far as Lord North's mission is concerned. I must confess, my dear fellow, that I was both hurt at your rather pointed and barbed statements and somewhat fearful that they might prove to be true.

I write hastily to inform you that you may soon expect to hear very good news! I am no detective, and must confess that my talents for spying have not been developed by my earlier career—however, one discipline I have studied and pursued with alacrity, and that studying now stands me in good stead.

In a word, there is a member of the congregation, Humility Cooper, who is in the confidence of our friend Brewster. She appears to be quite an attractive girl, and perhaps intelligent, but I have taken dead aim upon Miss Cooper, and if she can withstand the wiles of this novice spy, she will be unique! Expect to hear from me by the next post more concerning the elusive Mr. Brewster and the decline and fall of Humility Cooper!

> Your most obedient servant,
> Gilbert Winslow

Note his rather careless confession and the lack of conscience as regards Gilbert's woman-chasing. This letter reveals just the right tone at this stage of his life.

I use several letters in *The Honorable Imposter* in this way. Humility Cooper is a private person, not at all likely to blurt out all her feelings. She is also sensitive, too much so, perhaps.

Following are two letters Humility writes to her friend back in Leyden, a girl named Hope Stewart. She is, of course, aware that the letters cannot be posted until the first ship arrives from England and returns, so these letters are somewhat in the nature of a journal entry.

At the time of the first letter, she bitterly hates Gilbert Winslow. But it is in the writing of this letter that she actually lets herself confess it.

My dear Hope, there is no way to mail this letter, of course, but one day a ship will come and bring it to your door.

The men started building our houses on December 25, and although the weather was bad the next day, on Wednesday and Thursday, all was clear and the party was back at work.

It was decided to assign unmarried men to each family to save time, so there will only be 19 houses, the size of the plot adjusted to the size of the family.

Building the houses is very difficult, not at all like at home. A foundation of stone must be laid, then an open frame erected. Trees have to be cut and trimmed to square sections with a broad axe, then finished with an adze. Are you impressed with my knowledge? I have been talking a great deal to a young man named Peter Brown, one of the strangers from London. He is not really a carpenter, but has done some work in that line. He is teaching me how to sharpen tools so that I can be of some help.

I can hear you say, "Oh, Humility, what does he look like? Is he handsome? Is he married?" Well, perhaps you would ask that last question *first*. He looks very well, he is not married. I might add, at the risk of being vain, he is the most eligible bachelor on the ship, and I would be blind if I had not noted the attention he pays to me. But I am not ever going to marry.

I find this hard to write, my dear Hope, but I have no one to talk to here. It is a great sin on my part, but I must confess it, even if just in this letter that may never be seen by any eyes other than mine—I have not been able to forgive Gilbert Winslow for his behavior toward me.

I have prayed and wept and tried to *feel* that I have forgiven him, for has not God said we must forgive if we would be forgiven?

The worst of it is that I hate him not because he planned to betray Mr. Brewster, which was the real evil. No, I just set it down—I hate him because he made me love him—and he did not love me!

Now, it is down, and I look at it, read the words. But, Hope, he had done me more wrong than he knows, for I gave him my love—my first love—and when the discovery came that he cared not for me, something happened deep in my soul. I do not know how to say it right, but I know that never will I be able to love a man again!

What does this letter reveal about Humility's feelings toward Gilbert? What does it tell about her feelings toward herself? How does this letter highlight the struggle between her love for God and her feelings for Gilbert? Is she always honest? Does she mean it when she says, "I will never marry"?

As you can see, there are levels of meaning, and we know Humility better than perhaps through any other manner of writing.

And the letter does *double duty*. We discover something about time and we sense the hard tasks that the pilgrims face. Used sparingly, the letter is an effective device in fiction.

And now, one last device to go with the exposition, the journal and the letter:

IV. Mini-Essays

The mini-essay is a type of description, but it can also connect scenes. It is a form of summary, but it does more than compress time; basically it is a *philosophic commentary* on a character or some social element in the book.

I used this method at one point in *The Honorable Imposter*. After several *scenes*, I wanted to slow the action down so that the next scene would be more vivid and at the same time add texture by revealing a picture of the world of the *Mayflower*.

The *Mayflower* was a little world, sailing through the rolling, trackless water much as a single star cleaves through the ebony blackness of space. There was a difference, however; the star had fellows (invisible though they were to the eyes), while the ship was solitary.

Bobbing like a cork on the tossing waves, she was smaller than the leviathan that sometimes surfaced close enough for the passengers to see the waterspouts. But though dwarfed by the miles that lay beneath her keel, by the sky that unscrolled blankly over her mainmast, and by the mighty ocean stretching in every direction, she kept a life and order running though the ship—an image of the macrocosm of the planet.

Captain Christopher Jones was the archetype ruler; master,

potentate, king, prince, emperor, congress, parliament, court. He ruled the little world with the power of an absolute despot, the Great Cabin no less the seat of authority than the Vatican or Buckingham Palace.

The ship was its own cathedral, chapel, monastery, nunnery; there were as many divergent views among the inhabitants of the bobbing little world as the babble of tongues in the larger one. From the dim, superstitious thought of Richard Salterne, common sailor, little better than a half-wit, who thought of God only as a sort of murky stew engulfing the earth—to the profound meditations of William Brewster, philosophies of God were as diverse on the little ship as were the staggering varieties of life that teemed beneath her keel.

The above passage offers a fresh look at the world of the *Mayflower*, not the scientific facts of length and weight, but a philosophic measurement. John D. McDonald in his Travis McGee series was a master of the mini-essay. McGee goes into a bar where he moves through a monologue of sorts. What does the bar in America *mean?* What sort of people go in there? And why do they go? It is a combination of sociological, psychological, and theological approaches. It is very effective.

So, you alternate between dramatic scenes with:

I. Summary
II. Journals
III. Letters
IV. Mini-essays

On every page you make a choice. Shall I *show* in dramatic scene or shall I *tell* in some form of exposition?

The choice is formidable—but the more you write, the easier the choice becomes. You will develop a feel for which is *right*. Trust me.

Exercises – Unit Three

∼ Exercise 1 ∼

The main character of a suspense novel, a man of thirty-four named Spence Hawkins, is a family man with three children. He is devoted to them. He is arrested on false charges and forced to spend two months in a miserable city jail awaiting trial. He has never gotten in trouble, never done time in jail, never been separated from his family. During his imprisonment he grows paranoid and bitter.

Write a summary covering the two months between his arrest and his trial.

∼ Exercise 2 ∼

Spence Hawkins keeps a journal during his imprisonment. Write four entries spaced out over the entire time.

∼ Exercise 3 ∼

Write three letters from Hawkins:
A. To his wife after one week in jail.
B. To his twelve-year-old daughter, Tina, after one month's imprisonment. Tina, humiliated by her father's incarceration, says she hates him.
C. To his pastor one week before the trial. The two months in jail have sapped his faith, and he writes a bitter letter asking how God could have let such a thing happen.

∼ Exercise 4 ∼

Write a mini-essay showing the jail as a microcosm, a little world (as I did with the *Mayflower*).

~

Point of View

Once in the ninth century a Japanese nobleman and his bride were traveling on a lonely road in the mountains near Kyoto. A man came up beside them, and after luring them into the deep woods, overpowered and bound the nobleman and then raped his wife. Then the robber, moved by the wife's plea, untied the nobleman and dueled with him until he killed him—at least, that was how the robber told it later. But the wife reported that the robber fled after the rape and her husband, filled with shame, begged her to kill him. She did so, intending to kill herself as well, but failed. Not so, said the nobleman who (speaking through a medium) claimed that he finally killed himself. A woodcutter who had witnessed the whole thing gave a fourth version.

This is the story of *Rashomon*, the classical text for the study of point of view. It was made into a movie by Akira Kurosawa, and was based on a short story by the talented Japanese writer Ryunosuke Akutagawa. Akutagawa, a student of English literature, probably found the source of his story in Robert Browning's *The Ring and the Book*.

The nobleman claimed he killed himself, the robber boasted that he killed the nobleman, and the bride insisted that she did it.

What are we to make of this? It is a question, of course, of point of view. *Through whose eyes should we see?*

In this chapter we will consider two main approaches to point of view:

I. The first person point of view
II. The omniscient point of view

One good way to get a firm hold on the anatomy of point of view is to imagine the Smith family having a picnic in a clearing—father, mother, and ten-year-old son. They think they are alone, but actually, another observer, a strange and mysterious Mr. X, is standing some distance away, at the top of a small hill, and can see and hear all that the Smiths are doing.

During the picnic Mr. and Mrs. Smith quarrel and he slaps her across the face. Fix this image clearly in your mind—the Smiths on a picnic, unaware that they are being observed by Mr. X who sees all and knows all from a distance. Now, we go look at the Smith family who represent:

I. The First Person Point of View

Each of the three individuals at the picnic present a possibility for a writer. Whose story shall it be?

Let's say you decide on Mrs. Smith. Instantly the task of *creating* Mrs. Smith begins. From a hundred possibilities, you choose to make her a bitter, complaining woman who resents her husband's low income and the lifestyle it forces her to live. Her father is a wealthy stockbroker. She married her husband because he was romantic and convinced her they would share a romantic idyllic life. She constantly reminds him of the man she could have married and makes their home the pits. How will you focus the plot if you tell the story from Mrs. Smith's point of view? She feels unappreciated, wronged, and injured.

"No, I think Mrs. Smith might be too full of self-pity. Mr. Smith—he will be much better." Well, now you have a wife-slapper and that implies a tough, heartless, and self-centered individual. He might have left all his romantic ideas (if he ever had any) long ago and now sees his family as an anchor holding him back from better things. Perhaps he is not basically a cruel man, and even sees himself as a patient person, but he's been pushed too far.

You might decide that Mr. Smith is too hard and tough, that you need a viewpoint character who is not so coarse. This brings us to the third possibility—the boy.

Western literature has a tradition of exceptionally successful novels through young eyes—young Jane Eyre, David Copperfield, Pip, Maisie, and Jim Hawkins, to name only a few. The child's point of view is fresh and offers a startling contrast to scheming adults. And in some ways, children are exceptionally perceptive.

Your *second* choice, after deciding whether or not to use the first person, is which first person. Mrs. Smith, who received the slap, Mr. Smith who gave it, or boy Smith who witnessed it—who shall tell the story?

What are the advantages of the first person point of view?

It might be better to first note the disadvantages. Many critics insist that it destroys the necessary detachment between the writer and his work. When this happens, the result is an ego-trip for the writer, a supercilious tone of voice that can grate on the nerves.

The first person point of view is limited, for you can only include those things which the protagonist experiences—and you can only express those things in the speaker's language. Ernest Hemingway insisted that American literature began with a book called *Huckleberry Finn*. This is not true, of course, but consider what an achievement this novel really was. Twain filtered the entire story through the mind and experience of a fourteen-year-old uneducated boy. He gets away with it by using Huck's innocence as a means of satire. He is, for example, completely taken in by the King and the Dauphin, and that scurrilous pair's cosmic hypocrisy is magnified as the reader smiles at Huck's gullibility. Mark Twain is the puppeteer, of course, or perhaps the ventriloquist who puts the lines in Huck's mouth that actually reflect his own hatred of sham and hypocrisy.

We read the first page, and we *like* Huck. He is simple, honest, innocent, and he never becomes cynical despite being exposed to hardships and phonies all along the Mississippi.

That is the great advantage of the first person—immediacy. We listen as a real human tells us his story. The reader can identify with the teller of his own tale, recognizing himself: "Why, *I've* done that myself!"

Consider *Jane Eyre*, for example; one cannot imagine that novel written from any other point of view. The center of the novel is Jane's relationship with Mr. Rochester. She is poor, plain, despised, while he is wealthy, attractive, and at the top of society. It is a triumph to the art of Charlotte Brontë that somehow we accept Mr. Rochester's falling in love with Jane, but an even greater miracle is Jane's turning her back on Edward Rochester when she discovers he has a living wife.

Brontë must have planned this renunciation from the beginning, for in chapter one Jane narrates her experience as a child with John Reed. Jane is a dependent living with Mrs. Reed, and is despised by the three Reed children—Eliza, John, and Georgiana. She describes her terror of John simply in a scene where he demands that she come out of her hiding place and face him.

> John had not much affection for his mother and sisters and an antipathy to me. He bullied and punished me; not two or three times in the week, nor once or twice in the day, but continually: Every nerve I had feared him, and every morsel of flesh on my bones shrank when he came near.... Habitually obedient to John, I came up to his chair: he spent some three minutes in thrusting his tongue out at me as far as he could without damaging the roots: I knew he would soon strike... and all at once he struck suddenly and strongly.

John continues to torment her, pushing her so violently that she strikes her head against the door and cuts it. At this point, Jane rebels and strikes him. She is punished severely, but we get a glimpse of the indomitable spirit that lies beneath Jane Eyre's mousy exterior.

Edward Rochester senses this spirit. Knowing that Jane was in love with him, he had openly courted a woman named Blanche. In the climactic scene, he sees her spirit flash out at him in a fiery speech with the same intensity she had displayed against John Reed as a child:

Do you think I am an automaton?—a machine without feelings? and can bear to have my morsel of bread snatched from my lips, and my drop of living water dashed from my cup? Do you think because I am poor, obscure, plain, and little, I am soulless and heartless? You think wrong!—I have as much soul as you—and full as much heart! And if God had gifted me with some beauty and much wealth, I should have made it as hard for you to leave me, as it is now for me to leave you!

Seeing the world through Jane's eyes, its disdain and injustice, makes the hurts more immediate than if a third person had reported them. The first person works with *Jane Eyre* because we need to suffer *with* her.

Let's look at another example. What do you make of the following speaker?

Call me Ishmael. Some years ago—never mind how long precisely—having little or no money in my purse, and nothing particular to interest me on shore, I thought I would sail about a little and see the watery part of the world. It is a way I have of driving off the spleen, and regulating the circulation. Whenever I find myself growing grim about the mouth; whenever it is a damp, drizzly November in my soul; whenever I find myself involuntarily pausing before coffin warehouses, and bringing up the rear of every funeral I meet; and especially whenever my hypos get such an upper hand of me, that it requires a strong moral principle to prevent me from deliberately stepping into the street and methodically knocking people's hats off—then I account it high time to get to sea as soon as I can.

This is, of course, the opening of that whale of a book, *Moby Dick*. It is a metaphysical, philosophical work, with long dissertations separated by long, boring lectures on the color of sharks or the tail of a blue whale. The author of this tale, Ishmael (I need not point out that name's symbolic weight to all of you who are Bible students), is not a scholar, but a happy-go-lucky sailor with a streak of humor and a touch of a poet in his soul. The first person viewpoint of Ishmael works well for this book. Just think if that mad, megalomaniac Captain Ahab had told the story; it would have sunk to the bottom of the sea of its own weight.

Moby Dick is concerned with deep truth, with philosophic depths, but Ishmael is not a philosopher, indeed, he is not even a strong moral man in the traditional sense. This is underlined for us in the scene where he meets Queequeg, the heathen idolater. Ishmael is forced to share a room with Queequeg, and the first night, after the pagan worships his idol, he invites Ismael to worship with him. Ishmael reflects:

I was a good Christian; born and bred in the bosom of the infallible Presbyterian Church. How then could I unite with this wild idolator in worshiping his piece of wood? But what is worship? thought I. Do you suppose now, Ishmael, that the magnanimous God of heaven and earth—pagans and all included—can possibly be jealous of an insignificant bit of black wood? Impossible! And what is the will of God?—to do to my fellow man what I would have my fellow man to do to me— *that* is the will of God. Now, Queequeg is my fellow man. And what do I wish this Queequeg to do to me? Why, unite with me in my particular Presbyterian form of worship. Consequently, I must then unite with him in his; ergo, I must turn idolator. So I kindled the shaving; helped prop up the innocent little idol; offered him burnt biscuit with Queequeg; salamed before him once or thrice; kissed his nose; and that done, we undressed and went to bed, at peace with our consciences and all the world.

Polycarp, one of the Church Fathers, went to his death rather than offer one fragment of spice to a Greek goddess—but Ishmael works it all out so that his idolatry is really a *good* act. Melville created him so that he could do just that. If he had been a strong moral character, he would have been better off personally, but it is his amoral stance that qualifies him as an objective observer and reporter of Ahab's mad quest.

In 1984 I sent off a proposal for a Christian detective novel. My first novel, *The Seven Sleepers*, hadn't made me rich, nor had it caused a rash of phone calls from publishers begging for my work. When I received a letter from Dr. Wendell Hawley, editor for Tyndale House Publishers, expressing an interest in the detective novel idea, I went to Hot Springs, got a cheap motel room, and didn't surface until it was finished.

The first question I asked was, which point of view? As an admirer of the hard-nosed private eye genre, I knew that the best of that school, Chandler, Cain, and lately Robert Parker, have all used the first person. So I chose first person.

More importantly, however, I needed a male viewpoint character who was tough on the outside but gentle and even compassionate on the inside. I felt that to have Delaney tell his own story would more effectively show these two facets of the character.

The book became a game of sorts—to keep the street-wise, tough-talking cop moving through the pages, while at the same time revealing the Christian disciple beneath that hard image. Delaney is half embarrassed about his newfound faith, at times poking fun at himself. In the first chapter he is on his way to a halfway house for addicts and says:

> Most of these places take in young addicts and are operated by ex-dopers, usually pretty young themselves, and a lot of them are ministers of some sort. What I'm saying is that I'm the director of the Vine, and it makes me feel about as out of place as a bullfrog on the freeway with his hopper busted. It's good for a laugh around the precinct, and I get all the nicknames like "Padre" or "Preacher" not to mention "Holy Joe."
>
> Most cops get pretty hard, and only a few that I've known have any religion beyond the annual Easter visit or an occa-

sional Christmas Eve service. I guess the same could be said of jockeys, truck drivers, and roughnecks. Up until a year ago I had no more religion than a groundhog. Then something changed and I found myself saying, "I'm a Christian." It would be no surprise to me if someone stood up and denounced me for a phony.

Delaney speaks that last sentence to himself. The first person shows us in this case what Delaney would never voice—his doubt and sense of inadequacy. Now look carefully at two examples of how the first person point of view can reveal a character's *motivation* in a way that another point of view couldn't.

A young woman named Gina asks Delaney to find proof that her brother-in-law, convicted of murder and on death row, is innocent. Delaney knows the case and says harshly, "I hope they fry the sucker till his eyeballs crackle." And he means it, for the murder was terribly brutal. He turns to leave, when Gina's nephew Elvis comes in looking for her. Something about the boy causes Delaney to pause. Gina sends Elvis out, and Delaney questions the girl. The boy has leukemia, he discovers, and suddenly Delaney says, "I'll go see your brother-in-law." His sudden change of mind confuses the girl, and would confuse the reader if it were not for one fact that goes through Delaney's mind:

I couldn't tell her that Elvis was the same age my own boy would have been if he had lived. And I couldn't tell her it was my fault he was dead. And I couldn't tell her that Elvis had that same piping voice, and the same easy way with adults that I had begun to see in Scott before he died.

We don't get this secondhand from a narrator; it's a cry from Delaney himself. And in the next chapter when Delaney goes to see Gina's brother-in-law, he makes another decision out of keeping with his tough image. He discovers that the man was probably framed by a clever operator. But what can he do? The evidence is conclusive, the execution close at hand. A genuinely hard-nosed man would shrug and walk out, but once again Delaney behaves according to his inner values. The tone in the next interior dialogue is in the wise-guy voice that Delaney uses most of the time. It is as if he were laughing at himself for trying to buck the system, but as a Christian he is forced to try:

> Somewhere there was a guy spending fifty big ones. He was driving a Lincoln, eating at Cajun's Wharf with the bunnies that swarm to the loot. He slept good nights, and if he ever thought of the poor slob that he had maneuvered into Death Row at Cummings, he probably got a kick out of it. I could almost see his face—sleek, well-fed, glowing with success and health.
> And I was going to nail him to the wall!
> Or so the impulse took me. I have these little fantasies sometimes. Often I am John Wayne leading the troop to the last survivors of the wagon train before the savage Apaches make pincushions out of them. Then again, I am Batman with trusty Robin at my side, righting all wrongs. This Walter Mitty aspect of mine is usually kept carefully hidden from the public, for I have several puckered scars—results of terminal idealism!

When you use the first person, you must not "think" in your own voice. The voice is definitely that of Ben Delaney, not Gilbert Morris.

I am not a policeman. Huck does not sound like Mark Twain and Pip does not sound like Dickens. As a writer you must learn a new language, one deliberately tailored for your character.

II. The Omniscient Point of View

You remember the old story of the 450-pound gorilla? When someone asked where he slept, the keeper said instantly, "Anywhere he wants to!"

Mr. X is like that. He can do anything he wants to. Look at just a few of the miracles he can perform:

A. He can be objective as he tells the story. He can show-but-not-tell.

B. He can use any character's point of view.

C. He can comment on his own story.

D. He can take a panoramic view, moving through time and space.

E. He can reveal multiple facets of the characters.

As you can see, the omniscient point of view is versatile and flexible.

As I plotted *The Gentle Rebel,* Number Four in *The House of Winslow* series, I considered writing it in the first person point of view. A single short item in an American history textbook inspired the plot: "Deborah Sampson, a girl of eighteen, served for three years in the Continental Army of George Washington disguised as a man."

My first thought was *"She must have been the ugliest woman who ever breathed to pass for a man in a bunch of soldiers for that long!"* But the possibility kept gnawing at me, and finally I wrote the novel with that as a basis for the plot.

I had written all of the other books in the series from the omniscient point of view, but it occurred to me that letting Deborah (whose name I changed to Julie) tell her story would be more vivid.

But it never happened; I decided to use the omniscient point of view, after all. Why did I make this decision?

Because the first person narrator would have been too limiting. The book has a sub-plot involving a young man named Nathan Winslow. Julie, in the first person viewpoint, could not possibly know all the details of Nathan's life.

The following examples show how the omniscient point of view can *almost* give the immediacy of a first person narration. In the first scene of the novel, Julie is in her bedroom, terrified as she hears her uncle's footsteps. He is a brutal, sensuous man and the scene must convey her fear effectively enough for the reader to accept her running away from home. Here's the first scene as it appeared from an omniscient point of view:

If Julie Sampson had been born two years earlier or two years later, she would not have been in such a trap—or so she thought as she stood trembling in her small room, her back pressed against the wall.

If I were only 12 or 13, he'd leave me alone—or if I were 17, I'd be old enough to leave here!

She held her breath as heavy footfalls sounded on the stairs, came down the hall, then stopped abruptly outside her door. She suddenly pressed the back of her hand against her mouth to shut off the cry of terror that rose to her lips. The silence grew thick, so thick that between the solemn tickings of the clock she thought she could hear heavy breathing. Her eyes were riveted on the door as she waited for the pewter knob to turn. When the thought of escape through the small window beside her pierced her mind, she cast a quick glance at the snow that was drifting gently outside the glass.

She edged cautiously to her right. *I wonder if I would break my legs on the cobblestones?* she thought fleetingly, looking down at the walk that ran in front of the shop. She didn't really care— all she wanted to do was escape. She touched the catch on the window; then suddenly the footfalls retreated, going down the hall, and echoing down the stairs.

"Thank God!" she breathed, and then discovered that her legs were trembling so violently she could hardly stand, let alone make the jump to the walkway below. Dropping into the chair beside the small oak table, she hid her face in her hands and tried to think. She struggled to choke back the sobs that rose in her throat; finally, with great effort, she shook her shoulders, rose from the chair and walked to the washbasin at the foot of her bed. Dashing her face with cold water, she dried it with a thick, white cloth that hung at the end of the stand, then began to pace back and forth. Her mind whirled, filled with insistent but ineffective thoughts. She couldn't seem to sort them out, and any prayer she tried to utter seemed meaningless, an empty formula, a ritual learned from childhood.

This scene is shown from Julie's point of view, but it is not in the first person. In the same novel I develop scenes from the point of view of Nathan, the protagonist. That is the nature of the omniscient point of view.

Would the scene work more effectively if written in the first person? See what you think.

When I heard his steps, I dropped the book I'd been reading and moved to the back wall and stood there holding my breath—and the thought raced through my mind: *If I were younger he'd leave me alone—or if I were older, I'd run away!*

I prayed that he'd go by my door—but I knew he wouldn't. He always stopped there—and I knew that the time would come when the knob would turn and he'd come in. It was so quiet I could hear his breathing, and suddenly I moved to the small window and looked down at the cobblestones below. I stared at the knob, and if it had moved, I would have thrown myself out the window if it had killed me!

But then, thank God, he moved away, and my legs seemed to give way. I half fell into the chair and the tears that I'd choked back flooded my eyes. I choked back the sobs, pressing my hands against my mouth—and finally I got up and washed my face with cold water. I walked back and forth, trying to pray—but it didn't make any sense. The fear had drained me as it always did, and thoughts and prayers beat around inside my head like birds trying to get out of a cage.

The details are sharper in the first version, and the knowledge of Julie's thoughts in direct form has the same effect as a first person narration.

The first person point of view gives you a close, intimate look at one person. But it *limits* that same sort of look at other characters. Both methods have limitations, so make your choice and live with it.

Finally, watch for two tendencies that could creep in to spoil your use of the omniscient point of view.

A. Avoid making too many changes too quickly. In a scene, stay with one character at a time; don't jump from character to character as in the following abomination:

> Jerry sat beside the car, disgusted with himself and everybody else, wishing with all his heart he had stayed at the hotel. As he sat there with his head down, Marge stared at him, thinking how he'd changed. *He didn't use to be such a wet blanket,* she thought in disgust. Standing across the road watching the couple, Frank shook his head, wondering why she'd ever married such a wimp.

This is confusing and awkward. It drags the reader around by the scruff of the neck, and shouts, "See what *she's* thinking? And now look at him!—And what about *that* other guy, thinking like that?"

B. Create your characters' speech and thought patterns so that they sound like themselves, not like you. I stressed watching out for this second error also in the unit on character development.

The important thing is that you're comfortable with the point of view you've chosen. You might have to play around with both first person and omniscient to see which one fits your story.

Exercises – Unit Four

Situation: A family quarrel has taken place—a bad one. The setting is in a park with a playground. The husband (Mack, age twenty-eight) has just struck his wife (Ann, age twenty-four). It is the first time he has ever done this, though they have had many quarrels. Their son (Mickey, age eight) runs at his father and begins to strike him. This enrages Mack who whips off his belt and begins to beat the boy. Ann grabs their son and tries to run away, but her husband grabs them both and marches them away, cursing all the time.

⌒ Exercise 1 ⌒

Write the scene from Mack's point of view, in the first person.

⌒ Exercise 2 ⌒

Write the scene using an omniscient point of view.

Character Development— Appearance and Speech

Although the task of bringing your character to life is a formidable one, you can boil it down to four fundamentals.

I.   Physical description—what he or she *looks* like.
II. Speech—what he or she *sounds* like.
III. Behavior—what he or she *acts* like.
IV. Psychological patterns—what he or she *thinks* like.

We will discuss the first two in this unit and the other two in the next unit.

The average writer can do *one* of these things well, but the discerning editor can read one chapter and know immediately whether or not the writer is one who can keep *all* the balls in the air at the same time. All four elements *must work at the same time* for the character to reach three-dimensional proportions.

The bones must not show. I remember the student who handed me the rough draft of her novel with the comment, "I've written the book; now all I have to do is go back and put the descriptions and symbols in." She was crushed when I pointed out that those things are *organic*. The writer must build them into the work as it is created—not tack them onto the finished product like one would put a cherry on top of a chocolate sundae.

All four requirements for creating a believable character must flow together into a seamless whole and it doesn't happen automatically. Read William Butler Yeats' poem "Adam's Curse," on the nature of art. The poem is a conversation between the poet and a beautiful woman. She points out that her beauty is not easily achieved. She spends hours preparing herself, but she insists that this labor *must not be evident.* The poet instantly answers that poetry is exactly the same: "It's certain there is no fine thing / since Adam's fall but needs much labouring."

That chapter that your reader breezes through must have been birthed by your sweat and tears. Remember that *lazy writing makes for difficult reading; careful writing makes for easy reading.* Don't make your reader struggle through your writing. Present each character so forcefully that your reader hears his voice, observes his dress, eavesdrops on his thoughts, listens to what others think of him, laughs at his foolishness, and enters into his grief.

If you do any *less* than this, your character will be *flat*, like a paper doll. Turn him sideways and he'll disappear. Think about your favorite literary characters; you know them *as you know your real life friends.* They are believable because their creator has given them depth.

That is what I've designed this unit to help you do—*develop* a character. If you will master the four elements of this art, you can quickly learn to spot a flat, watery character in your own work as well as in the writings of others.

Throughout this unit, I will use the two major characters in my novel *The Indentured Heart* as examples. This novel is the third in *The House of Winslow* series. The plot covers a long time span, therefore the character development is more complex.

Following is the plot summary. As you learned in unit one, the story comes first.

Plot Summary of *The Indentured Heart*

Adam Winslow is different than the other male descendants of Gilbert Winslow. The Winslow men are tall, fair, and strikingly handsome, whereas Adam is of medium height and dark like his mother. He does not have the Winslow quickness of mind, either, so he grows up with a sense of inferiority. He lives with his father, his stepmother, and his half-brother Charles (who has apparently received all the strong traits of the Winslow line).

The story begins when Adam is fourteen, and the first section of the novel traces his boyhood, a rather miserable experience. He doesn't fit in with his family, so is sent to live with a relative in Massachusetts. It is there that he becomes a pupil of Jonathan Edwards. He grows up to become a physically strong man, and a gifted blacksmith. As he reaches manhood, he is strongly attracted to Mary, the daughter of Jonathan Edwards.

He goes to England on the first responsible business his family entrusts him with and his generous nature leads him to bring back a fourteen-year-old girl named Molly Burns. Molly is the abused daughter of a drunken brute. She comes as an indentured servant, bound to serve Adam until she is old enough to be free from her father's claims.

The second section of the book covers the next five years. Adam falls in love with Mary Edwards but has a rival in Timothy Dwight. Molly grows up to be a lovely young woman, but Adam can only think of her as a child. Molly gets engaged to a young man (mostly to make Adam jealous), and Mary chooses Timothy for her husband. As this section ends, Adam's brother cheats him out of his land, and Adam is forced to go to the Winslow land in Virginia.

Toward the end of this period, the final section of the book is set in the middle of the French and Indian wars, and Adam becomes a scout for General George Washington, going with him into battles. Adam also encounters the great evangelist George Whitefield and is converted to Christianity. While he is gone with the army, a British aristocrat seizes Molly and takes her to his castle-like home. It is during the struggle to get Molly back that Adam realizes she has taken possession of his heart. When he rescues her, the two are married.

Study this summary carefully, for you must learn to *build* your characters by looking at them on a lateral plane. By "a lateral plane" I mean you must see them in *stages*. When a parade passes by, you can see each float only *once* —when it passes by the spot where you are standing. But the observer in the Goodyear Blimp can see the entire parade; he can see each float as it begins the journey, watch it as it traces its way along the streets, and see it pass by the last spectator.

The Lateral Outline

You can view your story in the same way that the Goodyear Blimp views the parade. You can draw a *lateral outline*. I glue sheets of blank paper together to produce a sort of scroll, as long laterally as is necessary to contain the various stages of the novel. I write "Chapter One" on the far left side of the scroll, "Chapter Two" to the right of that, and fill the sheets with as many chapters as are in my chapter outline.

Chapter One	Chapter Five	Chapter Nine
Adam 14	Adam 17	Adam 20
very insecure	has matured	self-confident
shows signs of mechanical ability	physically, still has complex	expert blacksmith
no interest in God	hears Whitefield, begins to wonder about God	more interested in God, but still not ready to become a Christian

Along the left margin, I list the most important characters, leaving plenty of space in between names to identify the character development in each chapter.

Then, under each chapter heading, I list that character's personality at each stage in which the chapter takes place. For example, under chapter one, I list Adam's character traits at the age of fourteen, what he looked like, his family relationships, his hang-ups, etc. Just a few words for each, nothing elaborate.

My plot outline shows me how Adam *develops* over the course of the action. By the end of the book, Adam becomes a man of intense self-assurance. How? *Certain things happen to him!* These things are the plot details that you use to show how the character changes.

For example, Timothy Dwight, Adam's rival for the hand of Mary Edwards, is a historical character, and by all reports a giant of a man. No one could whip him in a fight. In chapter twelve, I bring Adam and Timothy together in a fight, and when Adam whips the huge man, it gives him a measure of self-esteem.

In the lateral outline, I listed details in every chapter that transform Adam from an awkward, shy boy into a strong, virile man, no longer haunted by his failure to live up to the Winslow standard.

Then I wrote under "Molly Burns" on the lateral outline: "Abused child. Crushed by poverty and hard times. Traces of beauty, but pale and thin. Cannot read. Yanked out of her home and thrust into a foreign culture." At the book's conclusion, Molly is a beautiful young woman of eighteen, accomplished and possessed of a firm character. How does this come about? In the lateral outline, I created situations which would cause her to develop. She becomes a student of Jonathan Edwards, for example, and Jerusha Edwards becomes fond of her as well, assisting her in the painful process of growing up.

The lateral outline is only for major characters; the minor ones do not need this kind of in-depth treatment.

If you learn how to use the four elements to develop your characters, inserting them into the lateral outline, you are well on your way to becoming a writer who can create.

The Character Analysis and History

You can't possibly remember details about all of your characters and keep them in your head. By the time you get to page 322, you will have forgotten the name of your heroine's hometown or if the small scar was on her left shoulder or her right. So it's important to make a character analysis and history for each of your major characters and some of the significant minor ones. Include birthdays, family members, physical description, psychological make-up, eccentricities in speech or manner, level of culture and education, and anything else that might come up in the story.

Following is an analysis and history I created for the heroine of my *Dani Ross* Series:

Danielle Lynn Ross
Age: twenty-six (April 11, 1964)
Height: 5' 8"
Weight: 135
Bone type: small bones
Hands and feet: perfectly formed.
Build: a little too full-figured to be a model
Face structure: oval or squarish, almost too square
Mouth: too large for real beauty
Eyes: grey-green, large and almond shaped
Nose: straight and rather short
Ears: small with large lobes
Coloring: fair, sunburns easily
Marks: small mole on right cheek; small white scar on neck just
    below left ear
Mannerisms: lifts chin when angry, sucks thumb when worried
Education: graduate of Tulane, accounting major, CPA
Special knowledge: crime (worked in Attorney General's office
    for two years); drama (college); horses (rides barrels)
Special abilities: memory expert, chess master
Family: Father is Daniel, a lawyer turned investigator; mother is
    named Ellen; one sister, Allison, age fifteen; one brother,
    Robert, age seventeen.
Personality: Strong sense of duty, doesn't trust emotion; wants
    to be logical; not demonstrative but would like to be; has
    always been smarter than other people and tries to play it
    down or hide it

History: Dani Ross was born April 11, 1964 in New Orleans. She graduates from high school at age sixteen (1980) and from Tulane at nineteen (1983) with a major in accounting. She works for one year at Davis and Company, a CPA firm, and gets her CPA in 1985. She starts law school at Harvard in 1986 and remains until 1988. In September of 1988 she drops out of law school and starts seminary. She falls in love with a student at Hayworth Divinity School, Jerry Hunt. He is a mission volunteer and inspires her with the vision of serving God by serving people. He dies in an automobile accident and she feels responsible. She decides to do what Jerry would have done if he had lived. She returns home to take over her father's investigative agency when he has a heart attack in 1990.

This may sound like a lot of work, and some of it you will never use, but it will save you time in the long run. Otherwise, you will find yourself constantly thumbing back through your work to find out the smallest details, such as if a certain character is seventeen or eighteen years old.

I. Physical Description—What He or She Looks Like

Think through the *details of a character's physical appearance so that they reflect his spirit.* Details in and of themselves are meaningless unless they add to the reader's emotional and intellectual union with the characters. Do not waste time on a multitude of details that fail to reveal what a character is in *essence.*

A. Physical structure. I reveal the root of Adam's inferiority complex as the book opens. He enters Ben Franklin's printing shop in Philadelphia with his father, brother and sister. We see them through Franklin's eyes:

He appraised the two tall men, both over six feet, noting the bright blue eyes and the blond hair with just a touch of red in the lamplight.... But the young boy was quite different—small and very dark.

This is like the first drop of rain. "... The young boy was different—small and very dark." The next drop comes in the next chapter. The Winslows are eating. Adam's stepmother, seeing the boy's dirty hands, says sharply, "Filthy! Why can't you be like your brother Charles?" Then comes this line: "Charles Winslow looked very much like all Winslow males—which is to say he was very handsome."

As Adam grows up, I refer to his "sturdy legs" and "well-developed upper body," all pointing to the man he will become. In chapter five, I create the following picture:

Adam wrapped the rifle in a piece of soft leather, then turned to face William. There was something slow and methodical in his movements, and though he lacked three inches of his brother's height, there was a thickness and breadth in his torso that William lacked. His chest swelled against the homespun shirt, deep and very broad, and there was a suggestion of power in every move he made. His thighs were heavy and his thick wrists and forearms swelled the sleeves of his shirt—the product of three years at the forge swinging a ten-pound hammer.

Adam's physical power is a reflection of the inner strength he attains by the end of the novel. Throughout the book I used detailed descriptions of his powerful body to give the impression of his growing strength.

B. Facial area. Think through the specific details of facial features, hair, and coloring. As a boy, Adam's appearance is mentioned early:

As he bent over, his coal-black hair fell over his eyes and he tossed it back with a sudden motion of his head. He hated his black hair and dark skin, and had cut his hair clean to the skull when he was only five. The fair hair and skin of the rest of his family stood out so that he felt like an outsider.

The "darkness" of Adam's hair and skin is a concrete detail, but it also emphasizes the psychological problem of insecurity that gnaws at the boy.

Usually it is best to describe a character's face in detail, but in this book I use instead Adam's strong muscular body as a symbol. I sprinkle the facial features, especially the eyes, around the book in single sentences.

"... There was a fire in his dark blue eyes that matched the coals in the grate."

"Adam's eyes were hard, harder than William had ever seen them."

"The thick cords of muscles in his solid jaw suddenly bunched up, and his eyes narrowed to slits of royal dark blue."

Other details, such as those that describe lips and facial shape, I throw in as part of the action. "Adam flushed, biting his full lower lip." "Adam nodded, and his square face was stubborn in the moonlight."

C. Clothing. The *kind* of clothing you put on your characters is important. Wearing a pair of jeans to a formal affair makes a statement about a person. The wearer is saying, "Look how free I am," which could mean, "Look how *rebellious* I am!" A woman who wears a revealing dress does not do so by accident; she is using her body to attract attention to herself, most often from men.

Adam's clothing is never flamboyant or colorful. "He was wearing a plain suit of brown, with a white linen shirt and a light blue waistcoat. His muscular figure gave that simple attire a certain air.... " The *lack* of fancy dress is an indication of Adam's personality. Plain clothes for a plain man.

The condition of clothing also makes a statement about your character. Tattered, worn clothing says "I am poor." Expensive clothing says, "I am rich."

In my novel *The Gentle Rebel*, clothing plays a critical role. This book follows *The Indentured Heart*, and Adam's son, Nathan, saves a young "boy" from freezing to death. Actually, the "boy" is Julie Sampson, a young woman who ran away from an abusive relative. In order to escape, she must maintain her disguise as a man. In the following passage, she takes the money supplied by Nathan to outfit herself.

She had given much thought to the matter of concealing her sex, but the old plan of merely covering up with loose-fitting, bulky clothes would not serve for this new life. Her quick mind had seen at once that she would have to dress like a clerk—but that meant wearing clothing much tighter and therefore more dangerous. All the time she had been choosing clothing, this had been in her mind and she had done well. She had, first of all, bound her upper figure tightly with a broad strip of cotton cloth ripped from her old clothes. Then she had donned the white stockings and a pair of buff knee breeches, the universal garment of young men everywhere. A light brown waistcoat, as loose-fitting as she dared, was buttoned up to where a white ruffle rose covered her slender throat. Over all this she wore a dark brown broadcloth coat with wide double lapels and white ruffles from a shirt extended past the cuffs. A pair of high-topped brown boots covered her slender legs.

What Nathan saw was a thin young man with eyes perhaps too large and features more delicate than most his age, but looking very well in a suit of new clothes.

Since the plot turns on the disguise, I needed to pay careful attention here to sharp detail. Once again, description must play a double role; it must tell something about who the person is internally beneath the external details.

D. Unusual physical attributes. Giving a major character at least one unique physical attribute can distinguish him from the other characters. Dickens was a master of this technique, often carrying it too far. In *The Indentured Heart*, Adam's stepmother slashes him across the face with a carpet beater, leaving a permanent scar on his cheek. His father, who has rejected him, is rebuked by the scar. "Now looking down, he saw that the puckered marks of the scar, which ran along the boy's lower cheek on the jawbone and continued across the neck, would always be a symbol of his own failure."

In the next chapter, Mary Edwards asks, "How did you get that scar on your face?" Adam responds at once: "Adam's hand reached up and covered the scar with an instinctive motion, and a quick anger shot through him."

· The facial scar is a symbol of the inner scar that causes Adam to feel inferior, and often he will try to hide it from people by covering it with his hand.

The character of Molly Burns is no less complex than that of Adam Winslow. Her appearance also changes as the plot progresses.

Molly appears first as a beggar on the streets of London, trying to get Adam to buy a handkerchief. Hardened to the infinite pleas of vendors and beggars, he is about to pass by, but she urges him:

"Oh, please, won't you tyke a bit of fancy work to yer lady, sir? Yer can 'ave it fer four bob."

He looked down at her, intending to shake her off, but paused when he saw the fatigue in her face. She had large eyes that looked gray in the fading light, and the smudges under the lower lids made them look larger. Her face was thin, her lips drawn with either pain or fatigue, and the finely-etched planes of her face with high cheekbones and a sweeping jawline did not seem to go with the ragged clothes that hung on her thin body. Most of the young beggars had faces blunted by ignorance and eyes dulled by the monotonous life of poverty they led; this girl, for all her rags, had something that was sensitive and delicate.

The above is a combination of language, physical appearance, and clothing. The next description of Molly comes after she has spent two years in America. Adam notes how she has grown:

> He marvelled at how she had changed. She had grown taller, of course, so that now at thirteen she was almost as tall as Mrs. Stuart. He thought suddenly of how much she was like the young colt that frolicked in the pasture across from the house— leggy, awkward, but with the grace that all young things seem to have. *First thing you know,* he thought with a sudden grin at her, *the place will be cluttered up with a herd of young fellows wanting to court her!*

Note the slight foreshadowing of the romance to come. Another passage quickly follows in which Adam looks at Molly as they prepare to leave for a party:

> Her eyes were blue-gray—Adam could never decide which— but the dark blue material of her dress brought out the blue. Her ash-colored hair was combed back into a single heavy strand, and was so thick and heavy that it seemed almost to pull her head back. Her figure was only just beginning to fill out— just a hint of womanly fullness in her straight carriage. She wore no jewelry, but the bright yellow ribbon that held her hair, and another at the high neckline of the silk dress, added a touch of color to her attire.

Again, note the combination of details—hair, figure, clothing. The next description comes several chapters later when she is fifteen:

> She pulled a gray cotton dress from a peg and slipped into it. The fact that it was too small made her realize how rapidly her figure had developed the past year. *Fifteen—and he still thinks I'm a child!*
> She looked down at herself, not at all happy that she was five feet nine—taller than any girl she knew and only an inch shorter than Adam. A year earlier she had begun to stoop try-

ing to disguise her height, but Beth had railed at her: "Sit up straight, girl—you look like a worm all bent over! God's given you a tall, strong body, and you go creeping around like a cowering slave!"

She had been bullied into a good carriage, but now she thought rebelliously, *Why couldn't I be small and dainty instead of a giant?* Then she stooped and peered into the small mirror on her desk.

What others saw was a face with rather high cheekbones, the planes sweeping down to a firm jaw totally feminine for all its strength. The eyes were calm, a strange blue-gray color, large and widely spaced. Thick black lashes curled over them, and the brows arched gently under a smooth broad forehead. Her lips were full with a hint of stubbornness, yet soft and red, and when she smiled, a dimple appeared on her left cheek, making her look almost saucy. When she let her thick ash-blonde hair down, it cascaded down her back like a smooth waterfall, but usually she wore it up in a crown of braids that framed her face.

The pale street urchin from London has blossomed into a beautiful young woman, but she is unhappy because she thinks herself too large for the man she is falling in love with. In the above description, we see the equivalent of Adam's facial scar. In Molly's own opinion, she is too tall, only one inch shorter than Adam. This unique aspect of her physical appearance plays a significant part in her development and in the plot.

By the end of the book, little of the street urchin is visible:

She was wearing a gown made of a light blue material, with lace at the bosom and around the hem. Her ash-blonde hair was lighter than he remembered, and her lips fuller. She smiled suddenly at him, and there was little left of the waif from London. This was a woman of twenty, with all the fullness of figure and mystery of expression one might desire.

In my descriptions, I treat Adam and Molly differently. Adam is not so finely drawn as is Molly. As a rule, clothing and fine facial detail are used to characterize women more than men.

As I said earlier, body type, facial description, clothing, and unusual physical attributes must be organic in your writing. That is why a lateral outline is so helpful; you can think these details through *before* you write your novel.

II. Speech—What He or She Sounds Like

If you are not careful, all of your characters will speak like one person; they will all speak like you. This is because the first words you think of for your characters to say will be your words. If you need to do this initially to get into the dialogue, go ahead. But be sure to go back and change it to the speech of that character. In the Winslow series, I had to continually go back and think, *Now, how would Adam say this—really?*

A. Quality of voice. Give each character a unique voice. Save the extremes, however, for your minor characters; i.e. a low pitched voice or a chronically hoarse tone. The reader grows weary when constantly reminded of such a thing.

As part of their character, Adam usually speaks quietly, and so does Molly. As a child, Adam was put down so often that he is still somewhat subdued even as he grows older. And Molly has the English quality of moderation in her speech.

B. Dialect. Molly speaks a cockney dialect when Adam first encounters her.

> "Oh, please, won't yer tyke a bit of fancy work to yer lady, sir? Yer can 'ave it for four bob!"
> "Sir, be yer goin' down ter 'auberk?"
> "That's me 'ouse, Mr. Winslow."
> "Miss Mercy, do yer think I can learn ter read?"

"Mr. Adam likes me now, but will 'e like me when I'm grown up?"

This grows old, so exercise restraint. *Any* dialect will irritate the reader if you use too much of it. Find ways to give the *flavor* of the dialect without using it extensively. In *The Indentured Heart*, Molly quickly loses her accent, and is soon speaking in an American fashion.

C. Pronunciation. Sometimes a character can pronounce a word or two in a distinctive manner so that his speech has its own "flavor." In one novel I read, the small town deputy pronounced "business" as "bidness"; "It's none of your bidness." Again, use this technique sparingly.

D. Authenticity. Every person has a certain way of speaking. As Mark Twain once pointed out, James Fenimore Cooper had a character speaking like a gilt-edge, tooled-leather lawyer out of Harvard on page 86, only to have him give a speech that would have shamed an illiterate Arkansas bootlegger on page 90. Adam Winslow would never use a word like "exquisite." He would know its meaning, but it would not fall from his lips. Molly Burns would never say, "I ain't got nothing to do." She studied with the family of Jonathan Edwards, and such phrases were rooted out of her speech patterns.

Fit each speech to each individual character. Adam grows into a strong man, and his speech is strengthened, as well. Molly matures into a strong-willed young woman, and her speech reflects that stubborn streak that lies beneath her attractive exterior.

We will continue the art of developing character in the next unit. Do the practice exercises until you are tired of them. Then rest up, come back to them when you are fresh, and do them again.

Character development is the most vital part of writing fiction.

Exercises – Unit Five

⌒ Exercise 1 ⌒

Using the model I developed for Dani Ross, create two characters. Write a character analysis and history for each.

⌒ Exercise 2 ⌒

Using the two characters you have created in exercise one, write a scene in which the two both appear.

The way they look and the way they speak should give the reader an idea of their personalities. For example, if one of them is dressed like a hippie, he or she probably *is* a hippie of sorts. If one of them speaks sharply and decisively, that tells the reader something about the character.

⌒ Exercise 3 ⌒

Write an interior monologue (develop a character's thoughts) and show the character's selfishness, even though the character himself is unaware of it.

⌒ Exercise 4 ⌒

Write a brief scene so that the character's speech reveals her personality.

Character Development—
Behavior and Psychology

John Steinbeck once observed his six-year-old son watching a western on television and asked, "How can you tell the good guys from the bad guys?"

"It's easy, Dad!" the boy replied. "The good guys wear white hats and the bad guys wear black hats."

Steinbeck wrote a fine critical essay entitled "How to Tell the Good Guys from the Bad Guys" in which he pointed out that poor fiction works like the early westerns. The characters are either "good" or "bad" with no gray areas. The hero and the villain are immediately identifiable. Later westerns carried on this tradition; who could ever confuse the heroic John Wayne with Lucky Ned Pepper?

It is not only low-budget westerns that employ this device. The Bard of Stratford, William Shakespeare, used the same method. (Not always, of course, for he was a genius at creating characters like Macbeth, a strange mixture of nobility and greed as well as many others who wore either a black or a white hat but changed them from act to act).

In his play *Richard II*, the chief character steps out on the stage and speaks to the audience. Richard was deformed, and he points this out at once:

I, that am rudely stamped, and want love's majesty
To strut before a wanton ambling nymph;
Cheated of feature by dissembling nature,
Deformed, unfinished, sent before my time
Into this breathing world, scarce half made up,
And that so lamely and unfashionable
That dogs bark at me as I limp by them. . . .

His deformity is so terrible that he believes no woman will ever love him. Then he looks straight out at the audience and *tells them exactly what he is going to do:*

And therefore since I cannot prove a love
To entertain these fair well-spoken days,
I am determined to prove a villain.

Richard says, in effect, "I am wearing the black hat! You don't have to try to figure out who the bad guy is—you're looking at him!"

Shakespeare's Richard II may be a wicked man, but he is not a *flat* character. He is one of the most fascinating villains in all literature. He is, for example, deformed, but so charming and witty, that he can make people do almost anything he wants. He murders one man who stands between him and the throne, then proposes to his widow who is weeping over her slain husband's coffin—and successfully woos her. Not a lightweight!

However, it would be fatal for you to bring a character on stage in your novel with a footnote announcing: *This is the villain.* I call this the Zane Grey School of Writing.

As a boy (and even later, I confess) I read the Zane Grey westerns with much pleasure. Grey was a dentist who never traveled west of the Mississippi River, but he wrote about a romantic American West that some still believe in. His books are formula novels; they all follow the same basic format and bear no resemblance whatsoever to the historical West. He uses one hero, one heroine, and one villain over and over again. In one book the hero is named Laramie Nelson, in another, Brazos Keene, and in others, Lance Renfee, Buck Manners, Tex Williams, or Lane Cole; the name doesn't matter because they are all the same man. He is tall, broad-shouldered, slim-hipped, and has wide-spaced eyes in his tanned face. He is quick with a gun, handy with his fists, and an absolute gentleman around ladies. A noble son of the range.

Grey's heroines are beautiful, virtuous, and mindless, and they, too, change their names but not their nature from book to book. They do everything but wear a sign around their necks saying in bold print: Look at me! I am the heroine!

And who is that stranger with the dark face, the sneer on his thin lips and two guns tied down low on his thigh? It is no other than the hard-faced villain, Dirty Dan! I have read all of Zane Grey's books, over forty novels, and every villain has thin lips. Once the reader becomes aware of this fact, the first man who pops up in the book with thin lips is marked—the villain!

Zane Grey type novels were successful in their day, but today's reader is a bit more sophisticated, requiring more from fictional characters. This means that you must create rounded characters, not flat characters. Let's discuss those terms.

A flat character has only one dimension. He has no depth, nothing more to him than what you see on the surface. All novels have these characters; they serve a purpose. Let's say your protagonist hails a cab to make a trip across town, and you want to show that he is highly nervous or afraid. The cabbie (the flat character) becomes your medium. Instead of narrating that "Marlowe was nervous and afraid," the cabbie can dramatize Marlowe's condition. He might say, "Something wrong, Buddy? You look kind of shook up." You could liven this scene up even more with something like: "The cabbie, who had the face of a man who had escaped life on a small farm in Arkansas and was determined not to go back to it, took one look at Marlowe, and snarled, 'Hey, Jack, if you're going to throw up, get outta my cab, will ya? Ya look like ya just seen Jack the Ripper!'" You would never tell your reader more about this cabbie. He is what is called in drama a *spear carrier*, the term used for those actors who file on stage to compose the mob or crowd or audience, a faceless group of people whose sole purpose is to react in some way to the major characters.

Make your minor characters come to life, but do not attempt to make rounded characters out of them.

While you want to keep this kind of character flat or one-dimensional, you still want to give your reader more than just a blurred image. It is your job as a writer to *create*, and you can only cause an image to form in a reader's mind if you furnish the details. In my novel *The Gentle Rebel*, I include a scene which takes place in winter. The hero, Nathan Winslow, and his brother arrive in Boston after a hard journey, and are met by a man who is uncivil:

"Mister Winslow didn't look for you." A thick-bodied man with a face blue from cold and red from drink stared at Nathan, and there was some resentment in his clipped New England speech as he added, "Don't have no help this time of day fer unloadin'."

If the man had been more civil, Nathan would have helped unhitch, but he was bone-tired and both he and Caleb were half starved. "We're going to my father's house. How far is it?"

The big man's face flushed, but he said, "Three miles back down the old Turnpike—you must'a passed it comin' in—big white house with pillars." He gave them instructions in a grudging voice, then grinned sourly. "You'll have a nice little walk—may get there by dark."

This man never appears again in the novel, but he performs an important function; he provides the necessary authenticity to the setting. Use minor characters whenever you can to add an authentic feel to your background or setting.

The creation of minor characters is an art that calls for hard work and flashes of genius, but we will leave that for later.

A *rounded character* is one who is three-dimensional; he has multiple aspects to his personality. The difference between a picture and a statue has to do with the object's dimensional appearance. A photograph or a painting may reveal many details of a person, but when you turn it sideways, you have nothing! On the other hand, you can walk around a statue, examining different aspects of the work. The sculptor's art is three-dimensional, while the painter works only in two dimensions.

We often have a two-dimensional view of historical characters. We picture George Washington standing nobly in a boat crossing the Delaware or in some other heroic pose. Did you know he had wooden teeth? Did you know at the Battle of Monmouth he cursed worse than any sailor? Did you know he was so inarticulate that when he was named General-in-Chief of the Continental Army he got up and left the room without saying a word? An authentic novel about Washington should include details such as this.

In unit five you learned that a character's physical appearance and speech can develop *roundness*. In this unit, we will look at the other two facets of character development:

III. How a character *acts* (behavioral patterns)
IV. Why a character acts (psychological patterns)

In time you will feel comfortable combining all four elements of character development to create a fully rounded character. But for now, remember to concentrate on *one* element, not two. Study each of these elements of character development carefully. Once again, I will use my novel *The Indentured Heart* to illustrate the principles.

III. Behavior—What He or She Acts Like

A. Your characters must act realistically. Unless your novel is a fantasy, your character's behavior should reflect real-life behavior. It was said of Shakespeare: "He held the mirror up to life."

Have you ever read a story where the character behaves like no human being ever did on this planet? In the first of my Barney

Buck novels I fell into this trap. The editor wrote back in irritation: "For crying out loud, Gilbert! These are kids with snotty
noses! Have one of them throw a temper fit or spit up or do something or other less than perfect." Mark Twain grew irritated with
children's stories in which the young are always portrayed as
angels instead of human beings. In reaction, he once wrote a story
called "The Good Child and the Bad Child," in which the good
child, who was perfect in every way, was struck by lightning and
died, while the Bad Child grew to be rich, happy, and successful.

Grace Livingston Hill, a Christian novelist back in the twenties
and thirties, created fictional characters that remind me of Nor-
man Rockwell's paintings; they portray a world we would all like
to live in, but which does not exist. She used the same viewpoint
character over and over, a young girl who is mistreated and has a
horrible time, but she has faith in Christ and always lives happily
ever after.

Christians come in all sizes, ages, and colors, but none of them
are made of stainless steel. If one took these characters seriously, it
would appear that Christians never lose their temper, never fall
into sin, never deviate from the Ten Commandments or the
Sermon on the Mount. This is a terrible misconception and it is
the writer's responsibililty to never mislead the reader like this.

In Arthur Miller's play *The Crucible*, the main character, John
Proctor, has been unfaithful to his wife (which he utterly regrets)
and is lacking in social graces. He has little more than formal religion, and possesses none of the inner warmth of several of the
other characters. The crisis comes when he either has to accuse
innocent people of witchcraft, or refuse and be executed. It is a lot
to ask of a man, to die for an ideal, and John Proctor has not
shown himself a man of ideals. In the play, he suddenly decides to
give his life for others. He says, "There's your miracle, that a man
like me would be willing to die for others." This is weak characterization. Miller doesn't set it up, does nothing to foreshadow this
sudden nobility.

Gilbert Winslow reaches a similar climax in *The Honorable
Imposter*. He has given his word to betray Brewster and the pil-

grims. All he has to do is carry out the assignment. But when it comes right down to it, he can't follow through. He refuses and loses all the rewards promised to him. Did I prepare the reader for this moment?

When Gilbert is first asked to become a spy, we read:

> Winslow stood there, caught in a wave of passion. With all his soul he longed to enter into the service of Lord North. But—to be *a spy!* It went against the grain and there was a revulsion that stuck in his throat at the thought of worming his way into a group—then selling the group for gain!

In chapter four, he leaves to carry out his assignment, but he is reluctant:

> Gilbert stared at Tiddle and finally gave a tight grin, saying in his husky voice, "Well, now that I've sold my soul, when may I expect to gain the whole world, Lucas?"
>
> Tiddle laughed, but there was a note of sadness in his face as he looked at Gilbert. "I'm a little sad to see a young man like you sell his soul for a mess of pottage, though."
>
> "A mess of pottage!" Gilbert exclaimed, then grinned at Lucas. "Why I'm getting a much higher price for my soul than that."
>
> Tiddle stared at Gilbert for a long time, then said, "Well, I trust you will enjoy your bargain—but it may be more expensive than you think now, Gilbert Winslow!"

All the way through the first section of the novel, Winslow struggles with his conscience, his guilt, so that when he actually does refuse to carry out his part of the bargain, it comes as no surprise.

The character's inner struggle evolves because of *motivation.* People act and speak, not out of a vacuum, but because of certain forces once exerted on them. A man will die for his friend because he loves him. Love is his motivation, the reason he chooses to die.

Every work of drama or fiction must contain this. Macbeth does not simply say one evening, "I think I'll kill the king tonight." The first section of the play dramatizes *why* he decides to kill his king. And in your novel, your characters' major decisions and actions should occur, not out of some vague impulse, but out of the forces that have drawn them to be who they are. This is what character *building* is all about.

Just as you use motivation to develop your good characters to act nobly, never paint a villain all black. Just as your hero's flaws create sympathy in the mind of the reader, so does adding a touch of kindness make your villain's evil stand out. We know that Hitler loved dogs and Mussolini made the trains run on time.

In the creative process, I can tend to forget that none of us wears white hats all the time, nor black either. So often in the process of revision, I add a touch or two here and there to make a character more realistic. If our fiction is to hold the mirror up to life, we must show both the smooth and the rough edges in our characters.

B. Your characters must act *consistently*. By this I mean they must stay consistent within their own world, the novel they inhabit. If you carefully build up a character as kind and loving in the first ten chapters, do not transform him suddenly into a selfish monster in chapter eleven.

"But that sort of thing happens all the time!" you protest. "Why, I read about a man over in Baker last week who was a good husband and father for twenty years, yet all of a sudden he embezzled money from his company and ran off with a dizzy blonde!"

The truth is, he did not steal and abandon his family *all of a sudden*. He may have taken the money, jumped into a car and actually left town in half an hour, but he worked up to that shameful act over a period of weeks, months, or even years. If you were writing that scenario into a novel, you would first show him as a loving husband and father, and a hard-working employee. At the same time, in chapter two you would begin to show that underneath that image, he was unhappy. He would begin his affair with the woman in a "small" way, almost innocently. Then he would build up the flirtation in his mind. It would progress slowly until it turned into an adulterous affair. There is no suddenness about such things; they develop and incubate over a long period of time in our lives, and you must take the character through the various stages step by step. It is your job to provide the necessary *motivation* for the character to act as he does.

In James M. Cain's novel *Double Indemnity*, the protagonist is not a particularly moral man except in the matter of his work. He is an insurance investigator and knows full well that most murderers who kill to collect on insurance are caught and executed. At the beginning of the book, he is a man who would never fall into that trap.

But he does.

Slowly, slowly, he is drawn into just that trap, and Cain does a masterful job of bringing certain incidents into the plot which finally lead to the fateful moment where the investigator says, "You're going to kill your husband—and I'm going to help you." By the time he says this, however, it is not inconsistent for him to plan a murder; he has changed.

Always prepare the reader for your character's actions or he or she will appear inconsistent. Jane Eyre, starved for love and desperately in love with Mr. Rochester, leaves him at once when she discovers that he is married, but this comes as no shock to the reader, for throughout the book, Brontë develops a woman who will do the right thing no matter if it costs her the person she treasures most in life. Showing goodness in fiction is difficult. If one is not careful, the character comes across priggish or sentimentally sweet.

Jane Eyre must take her stand, for this is the most critical moment in her life and in the novel. Mr. Rochester has no scruples against adultery. He tries to convince her to live with him without marriage and asks, "Who in the world cares of *you*? Or who will be injured by what you do?"

Jane replies with a speech that would sound false and pompous in the mouths of most characters:

> *I* care for myself. The more solitary, the more friendless, the more unsustained I am, the more I will respect myself. I will

keep the law given by God; sanctioned by man. Laws and principles are not for times when there is no temptation: they are for such moments as this—there I plant my foot.

Have you ever read a better dramatic statement of Christian faith? It only works because over the course of the novel, Brontë has worked hard to develop the kind of woman who *could* make such a statement. Could Jane have said, "Very well, Mr. Rochester, I will live in sin with you"? This would have violated every detail that Brontë employed to create a woman of integrity.

I mentioned earlier that your characters must act in a consistent manner. The exception is the character whose trait is *inconsistency*. Some people are truly unstable, and you may have reason to create a character who is plagued with this. In Charles Dickens' *Bleak House*, one of the major characters is young Richard Carstone, and despite the fact that he is charming and lovable, his character is built on inconsistency. He changes with the morning sun, and it is this very trait that brings about the tragedy of the novel.

C. Your characters must have mannerisms. Develop your characters' gestures and mannerisms so that they indicate something about the action or the character himself.

For years I have worn glasses, and I have the annoying habit of shoving them up my nose with my forefinger. When I got my Ph.D., my wife was sitting so far back in the stands she could not identify me. (We were look-alike penguins in our black robes.) Later she said, "I couldn't see your face, but I knew you were the one who was always shoving at your nose with your finger."

Adam Winslow's facial scar is a mark of shame to him. When he gets confused or embarrassed, he often raises his hand and covers it up. In the same book, Molly has a tendency to slump, evidence of her feeling that she is too tall to be attractive. Who could ever forget Captain Queeg in *The Caine Mutiny* rolling his steel ball bearings around every time he was threatened?

Bodily postures are clues to character and attitude. Certain studies show that real communication in any social exchange is about 35 percent verbal and 65 percent nonverbal. Let your reader see the tics, the shifting eyes, the tightly clenched fists, the lip-biting, and all the other signals that accompany talk.

D. Your characters must have activities. Your character has a life not necessarily connected to the plot. If he is a detective, he will spend some of his time in activities unrelated to solving crime. For example, Nero Wolfe raises orchids for a hobby.

"But why should I bring things like this into my characterization?" you ask. It's part of creating a three-dimensional character. The heroine who raises prize quarterhorses and is an avid reader of Civil War history has more depth. Robert Parker's hard-nosed detective, Spenser, is an expert cook. Somehow that fact shocks us, that a man who shoots people and beats them up with abysmal regularity can put on an apron and whip up a delicious meal. It is incongruous, but that kind of incongruity adds another dimension to your story.

E. Your characters must have *reactions*. When someone drops a ten-pound Stilson wrench on his toe, he will react. That reaction will not reveal what he would *like* to be, but what he actually *is*.

The Indentured Heart focuses on the relationship between Adam Winslow and Molly Burns. I spent the first five chapters of the novel preparing the reader for chapter six. It took that long to develop Adam so that his reactions are believable. He has gone to London with the money to buy equipment. This is the first time his family has trusted him to do anything, so it is highly important to him that he do well. In chapter six, he forfeits the opportunity to gain his parents' approval when his reaction to Molly's mistreatment causes him to whip her father then spend all the money to pay the man off so that she can accompany him to America as an indentured servant.

Was this reaction out of character for Adam Winslow? I don't think so, for throughout the book I planted hints of Adam's generous nature and his physical strength. Even before he goes to England he becomes a father figure to a child of Molly's age. He writes to her from England:

I have told you quite a lot about the Burns family. Molly is your age, but you would find her quite ignorant. She cannot read a word, but she delights in books. I wish she could spend some time in your company, Mary, for she is a warmhearted and loving child who could do well if she had the opportunity.

Alas, there is no chance for that! Her mother is a good woman, but worn out with work and dominated by her husband. I can say nothing good about *that* one, for he is a brute who lives on the labors of his wife and children. Worse, he mistreats them frightfully!

I have seen the bruises on Mrs. Burns and on the children and pray that I will never be present to witness the thing! I had an awful battle once with a man who was mistreating his dog, and I do not think I could stand to see a woman or a child beaten!

That last paragraph should prepare the reader for Adam's reaction. He is present when the brute mistreats Molly and instantly leaps to her defense. His decision to spend the equipment money on her indenture is part of that reaction.

Isolate these five aspects of your character's actions and work on each of them, but remember, they are all part of the whole and the reader must not see the bones.

IV. Psychological Patterns—What He or She Thinks Like

Why a character acts like he does in a given situation is a quite different thing from what his actions are. Several years ago, a book was released titled *Why Am I Afraid to Tell You Who I Really Am?* It centered on our tendency to hide what we are at times by a veneer. Two of Dickens' minor characters are a couple named "Veneering." You can imagine what he did with them.

Use the following five tools to reveal what a character is beneath the external:

A. His or her basic psychological makeup
B. His or her past

C. His or her psychic wounds
D. His or her self-image
E. His or her image, as seen by others

These methods overlap, and you will not use all of them, of course, but consider each of them when you create a major character.

A. His or her basic psychological makeup. According to medieval scholars all men were composed of four elements which they called "humors." Each of these gave a man a certain temperament. If these were in balance, a person would act normal, but they hardly ever were. If, for example, someone possessed an overabundance of a certain physical element, he was "choleric." Given to bloodshed, he would act out in violent ways. If he possessed too much of another element he would be listless and slow to act.

Modern psychology is more complicated than this, but we all have certain behavioral traits; we are quick to act, impulsive, or we are slow and cautious. Some are trusting, and others are suspicious. We see this in children; some are boisterous and noisy while others are quiet.

Why are we like this? Because God made each of us with a unique spirit. When you "create" a character, you are a sub-creator. You decide what kind of personality you will give each character. In *The Indentured Heart,* Adam and his half-brother Charles are radically different. Adam is slow-thinking, trusting, and unselfish; Charles is quick, egotistical, and manipulative.

I dramatized this early in the second chapter in a scene where the two are in the kitchen. Adam is in disgrace with his stepmother, and Charles rebukes him:

Charles was irritated. "You're so good at some things—and so dumb at others! If Mother had beat me as much as she has you, I'd think of a way to get out of it. That's the difference between you and me, Adam. I take better care of myself than that!"

Adam looked ashamed and mumbled, "I wish I wasn't so dumb!"

Charles shrugged, saying, "You're smart enough in everything except books—and learning how to look out for yourself. All you have to do, Adam, is find out what people want and give it to 'em. Then, when you get big enough you can tell 'em to jump in the river!"

Can you see the different psychological bents of the minds of the two boys? They are only thirteen years old, but each of them has a certain mind-set that will intensify as they grow older.

Later, when the boys' wealthy Aunt Rachel leaves the room, Charles says:

"Aunt Rachel sure does think a lot of you. Wish she liked me half as much!"

Adam stared at him in amazement. "Why, she likes you as much as she does me!"

"No, she don't," Charles said regretfully. He looked at the gold coin and added, "You can get more of these out of her, Adam. If you'd just butter her up, why, she'd give you 'bout anything you asked for!"

The idea had never occurred to Adam, and he stared at the coin in his hand, pondering the thought. Then he shook his head, saying, "No, she doesn't like me more than you."

Charles looked at the dark face of his brother with disgust. "You *are* dumb, Adam! You gotta' learn to watch people and when they can do you some good, why, you gotta' play up to 'em. It's the only way to get what you want, see?"

When I wrote the above scene I was anticipating the section of the story when Charles would manipulate Adam. When I reached that point, Charles' deception of Adam was believable because I had developed Charles' manipulative streak throughout the novel.

Do you see why I insist that character is plot? In this kitchen scene, the *character* of Charles is clearly seen, as well as is Adam's. Later on, when the *plot* depends on a certain *act* of Charles, plot and character become one. He acts a certain way because his character has a certain bent.

B. His or her past. Basically, all of us have the same experiences: childhood, school, family, friends made and lost, work, play. All past events in our lives shape and form who we are today. Out of this immense river in our characters' lives, we must select a few elements which will represent the whole. This is why I write at least a brief biography of any character that I think will play a significant role in the story and a complete biography for each major character. I might come up with something like the following:

> Thad Novak, born in the slums of New York in 1845. Father is a first-generation American from Poland. Mother is the daughter of a railroad section hand in the Boston area. Has two younger brothers and one older sister. Father paralyzed in an accident when Thad is six. Novaks scarred by poverty. Older sister goes bad, works in a saloon. At school the Novaks are ridiculed by other children because of their accents and shabby clothing. Thad longs to be like other boys, and early sees that money can buy the things he thinks are important. Goes to church some, a Lutheran church, and is befriended by the pastor, a young man just out of seminary. Thad falls in with evil company, and ultimately into crime.

This is the framework: family, school, economics, church. From this brief sketch, the details must emerge.

Several factors shape Adam Winslow's life. He is slower than his half-brother and lacks the family good looks. His stepmother dislikes him, and his father blames him for the death of his mother who died bearing him. Later in the book he goes to live with his brother who sincerely cares for him. He is taught by Jonathan Edwards and begins to gain some self-esteem. Then he fails his brother's trust by bringing home an indentured servant instead of the machinery he was instructed to buy, and once again he feels like a failure. In the years that follow he becomes a success as a blacksmith, and later in the book, becomes a trusted aide to General Washington in the French and Indian Wars. It is only as you create a past for your character that he can evolve into the person you want him to be in the present. The term often used for this creating of your characters' past is *back story*.

C. His or her psychic wounds. To a great extent we are also shaped by our difficulties. And sometimes our difficulties leave scars that are slow to heal. Most of the past experiences that form Adam Winslow's character are of a painful nature. Some people believe that a person's wounds are the basis of all actions that follow.

Suffering is truly redemptive in life, depending on how a person handles it. In Stephen Crane's *The Red Badge of Courage* we see this clearly demonstrated in Henry, the protagonist. Henry is a young soldier in the Union Army, and he has a dreadful secret: he fears that he is a coward. That is his "wound." Others seem to charge into battle with no fear at all, but Henry is tormented with the fear of showing the white feather. It is a psychological wound, and no less painful than a physical one. Indeed, Henry is envious of others who are shot, wishing ". . . that he too might have a red badge of courage." In the end he overcomes his psychological fear, and gets his physical wound.

Joseph Conrad's hero in *Lord Jim* deserts his post in a momentary spasm of fear, and the rest of the book is devoted to his attempts to redeem that one dark moment. He is only "healed" from that wound when he dies in a heroic fashion.

In Ernest Hemingway's *The Sun Also Rises*, Jake Barnes is rendered sexually impotent by a war wound. But that physical wound that bars him from physical love is only a symbol of the psychic wound that affects his soul—for Jake is a modern man who loses not only the power to love physically but the capacity to know love in any form.

A close study of a well-crafted novel is a study of the painfulness of human existence—a record of an individual's wounds, his attempts to find happiness in spite of them. In the Bible, after Jacob's wrestling match with an angel at Bethel, he was wounded in the joint and forever after walked with a limp. Give your character a wound, then let him either overcome it or let it destroy him.

Read *Great Expectations*, thinking about psychic wounds. Who are the characters and what are their wounds?

A. Pip is obsessed with a desire to get rich so that he can marry Estella. When his "great expectations" fail, he is ruined, and it takes years for the psychic wound to heal.

B. Estella is brought up by an eccentric relative, and taught to despise all men, to destroy them if possible. Small wonder that she destroys herself in the process!

C. Miss Havisham's fiance jilts her. She stores up hatred, celebrates it in her shrunken soul, and is finally consumed by her vain obsession.

D. Abel Magwich answers simply when asked how he was brought up, "As a warmit (varmint)." Born and reared in a criminal environment, he becomes a criminal. Ingeniously, Dickens transforms this man into the most gentle person, the most loving in the entire novel. He overcomes his past and his scars are healed by the time he dies.

D. His or her self-image. A character may be aware of his problems or he may deceive himself. Work on perfecting your ability to convey how *the character himself* becomes aware of what he really is. The reader usually sees and understands the character's limitations, but the fun is in *watching the character himself gain this rev-elation.* In *Great Expectations,* Pip is a snob, but he is unaware of it. Estella, on the other hand, possesses a clinical knowledge that her upbringing has rendered her incapable of love. Pip is almost destroyed when he finally becomes aware of his own obsession, and Estella, after years of painful experience, comes to realize that she is capable of love.

E. His or her image as seen by others. Our characters are constantly in touch with other characters; let the reader in on how these characters view one another. This technique has several advantages. You can reinforce development of a certain character from another point of view. You describe him as you see him, but others see him in a different light.

One way to do this is to let one character comment on another.

Another way is to include scenes in which the hero is absent, and bring his enemies onstage to talk about him. This can give the reader a sharper picture of the opposition. It can also enlarge your novel's stage, for it includes not just the protagonist's world but reminds the reader that multiple "worlds" are out there.

Work on these elements: appearance, speech, actions, and motivations.

They will never achieve exact *balance* between characters. One character will require more psychological development; another's actions bring her to life.

Be selective, for if you try to develop a character to too great an extent, you will soon clutter your story and lose your character under a mass of details. Study successful models and imitate them.

Exercises – Unit Six

⌒ Exercise 1 ⌒

In fifty words or less, explain the difference between a "rounded" character and a "flat" character.

⌒ Exercise 2 ⌒

Write a one-page character sketch and explain how you will bring this character to life, how you will avoid flatness. Use details. For example, you might say, "Jack Carmody has a terrible guilt complex that he will go to any length to keep hidden. It all stems from the fact that his younger brother drowned in a backyard swimming pool, and Jack's parents blamed him for it."

⌒ Exercise 3 ⌒

Outline briefly the factors that might lead to a character's greatest failure in life. List them in the following examples:

A. When he was seven years old, his parents were arrested for dealing dope. He never forgot this.

B. When he was twelve years old, he was excluded from membership in an exclusive club.

∼ Exercise 4 ∼

Create a character with a psychic wound. For example, two sisters are left with their terminally ill mother. Jane runs away and lets Sue stay home and handle the tragedy. You want to write about Jane. List five or six of Jane's mannerisms, habits, actions, and reactions. Maybe Jane avoids old people. Another character might ask her to go to a nursing home and she overreacts.

Unit Seven

Dialogue

I picture Daniel Defoe breezing right through the writing of his masterpiece *Robinson Crusoe*. There is no dialogue in the book!

Well, perhaps a little when Crusoe teaches Friday to speak—but 99 percent of the novel is Crusoe's journal, so Defoe was spared the constant necessity of trying to find some new way to say "He said."

And those dramatists don't have to struggle with that business either. With the exception of a few stage directions, the whole structure is dialogue—people talking to one another. Consider the first scene in *Hamlet* as Shakespeare wrote it:

Bernardo: Who's there?
Francisco: Nay, answer me. Stand and unfold yourself.
Bernardo: Long live the King!
Francisco: Bernardo?
Bernardo: He.
Francisco: You come most carefully upon your hour.
Bernardo: 'Tis now struck twelve. Get thee to bed.
Francisco: For this relief much thanks. 'Tis bitter cold. And I
am sick at heart.
Bernardo: Have you had quiet guard?
Francisco: Not a mouse stirring.

The novelist would have to struggle with this:

"Who's there?" Bernardo asked.

"Nay, answer me. Stand and unfold yourself," Francisco said.

"Long live the King," Bernardo said.

"Bernardo?" Francisco asked.

"He," Bernardo answered.

"You come most carefully upon your hour," Francisco said.

"'Tis now struck twelve. Get thee to bed," Bernardo said.

"For this relief much thanks. 'Tis bitter cold and I am sick at heart," Francisco said.

"Have you had quiet guard?" Bernardo asked.

"Not a mouse stirring," Francisco answered.

You see how awkward this becomes? "He said—she said—he said—she said—he answered—she asked—he said."

But the day of the journal-novel is gone, and fiction is not screenplay; therefore, all of us who plunge into the craft of fiction must master the art of dialogue.

In this unit I offer the five principles of writing good dialogue. This part of writing is deceptive; it seems simple, but as Yeats said, "Those move easier who have learned to dance." Writing natural dialogue involves several skills, and as with other elements of writing, it is like juggling several balls. Anyone can juggle one or two balls, but when the third is added, it complicates the feat. The five principles are:

I. Mechanics
II. Variety of Position
III. The Action Tag
IV. Variety of Length
V. Tone

I might suggest that you get a larger wastebasket, for the writing of effective dialogue is achieved only by lots of practice.

I. Mechanics

You might want to skip this section, but for those of you who took English many years ago, or who forgot to go to class when this facet of writing was being taught, I will review the basics of using direct quotations.

A. Enclose any direct quotation in double quotation marks.
1. John said, "I won't be back until tomorrow."
   The opposite of this is the indirect quotation.
2. John said he wouldn't be back until tomorrow.
   The first example gives John's *exact* words. The second reports what he said but not in his exact words.

This is the basic rule. You may encounter a few problems if you attempt to follow this rule though, and the next four points address these potential problems.

B. Use single quotation marks to punctuate a quote within a quote. When a character is reporting another character's exact words, punctuate the entire quote with double quotation marks, but set off the reported speech with single quotation marks.

Mrs. Jacobs said, "I have never forgotten that my mother once told me something about men. She said, 'Helen, never let a man kiss you on the first date.' And that is what I am telling all my daughters."

C. Place commas and periods *inside* double quotation marks. Place question marks, exclamation points, and dashes *either* inside or outside double quotation marks, depending on their function. Isn't this a hateful rule? But there is no other way to put it. Here is your basic rule: Put the punctuation marks inside the double quotation marks if they are punctuating the quoted material itself:

"Do you think it will snow?" she asked.
"Of course it will!" he replied.

Put the same punctuation marks outside the double quotation marks if they are punctuating an entire sentence rather than the quote within that sentence:

Was your father joking when he said, "I'm going to get a job"?

I've told you to stop calling me "Sweetie Pie"!

Now, try this:

Who was the naval hero who once said, "Don't give up the ship(?)"(?) Does the question mark go *inside* or *outside* the quotation marks?

Is the sentence itself a question? If so, then the question mark goes *outside* the quotation marks. Obviously the above sentence itself *is* a question; therefore, the correct punctuation is:

Who was the naval hero who once said, "Don't give up the ship"?

But what about this next example?

I know the famous man who once asked the question, "What will become of my poor country(?)"(?)

The sentence itself is not a question, but the section inside quotation marks is; therefore, place the question mark *inside* the quotation marks.

I know the famous man who once asked the question, "What will become of my poor country?"

D. Use ellipsis to show the omission of words from a direct quotation. This punctuation technique comes in handy for the writer of dialogue. Look at the following sentence:

1. "Well, I just can't be sure.... "

What happens at the end of that sentence?

The voice trails off. What you want to show is an indecisiveness, a hesitation in the speaker. An actor can simply let his voice fall away. To achieve the same effect, the writer uses ellipsis. Use it sparingly, whenever such a tone is essential. An ellipsis is three periods, plus one period to end the sentence for a total of four periods.

E. Use a dash to show a speech that is abruptly broken off.

1. "Not a one of us in this place would—look out!"

Obviously the speaker has spotted a giant rattlesnake about to strike, or perhaps a gigantic eye peering in through the window.

He breaks off his calm speech to yell; the dashes show this. In typing, use two hyphens for a dash.

II. Variety of Position

I referred briefly to the element of tags in the introduction of this unit. Now I'd like to show you how you can alternate the positioning of your speaker tags (He said, she said) to make dialogue move in a lively fashion.

A. Put the tag *before* the quote.
1. Lord Roth said casually, "I forgot to mention that a relative of mine—a distant relative—will be one of the guests tonight."
2. Gilbert quickly asked, "Oh, has she been seeing someone then?"

This is the weakest position for a tag. I thumbed through almost a hundred pages of *The Honorable Imposter* and found no more than five instances of this, and each of them employed a qualifying adverb—"Gilbert *quickly* asked...."

B. Place the tag *after* the quote. If you need to use a tag, in my judgment, the best place for it is after the quote.
1. "Good! I"m about to turn into a block of ice!" Cecily said with chattering teeth.
2. "He may be of more use than your average parson," Lord North murmured.
3. "Oh? And what about me?" Cecily asked quickly.

The tag is a literary device, and when it is stuck in front of the speech, the reader cannot miss it. But when it is placed *after* the speech, it seems to move more smoothly with the flow of the dialogue.

C. Place the tag *within* the quote.
1. "You can make any decisions you please," Lord North said,

"but whatever you decide I will have to approve."

2. "Lady Cecily," he said, "I must take my leave."

D. Place no tag at all on the speech. The only danger is in going too far with this method. In most cases, a tag is actually not necessary to identify a speaker. In the following section, there is never any doubt of the speaker's identity. I start off using action to identify the speakers, a technique we'll discuss in my next point. But then I move into using just the character's spoken words.

"My name's Winslow. I have business with Mr. Cushman."

"I'm Robert Cushman." A slight man dressed in brown cloth was standing beside the desk. He had a thin face, and a tic in his right eye drew up that side of his face from time to time. "You've come from Leyden?"

"Yes."

"I don't believe we've met," Cushman said with a trace of suspicion in his thin face.

There was a tension in the room that Gilbert didn't understand, but he needed to assuage any doubts if he were to get information. "I'm new to Green Gate, Elder Cushman. But you know my brother, Edward, I think."

The name had the power to remove all doubt, and Cushman smiled at once, stepping forward to offer his hand. "Of course, of course! How are things progressing at home?

"I have this letter from Mr. Bradford and Mr. Carver." Gilbert took the letter, slit the seal and read it.

"You know the contents of this?"

"No. I was coming to London on business and the elders asked me to bring it. It has to do with the voyage, I assume."

"Yes. In order to hire the ship to take us to the New World we must have a full company."

"Aren't there enough volunteers from the Leyden church?"

"Not half enough—and Mr. Weston has recruited a group to fill out our number."

"Are they of the Brownist persuasion?"

"Mr. Winslow, they're *nothing!* Why, already there's a name for the two groups—saints and strangers!"

A smile touched Gilbert's lips, and he repeated the phrase. "Saint and strangers—well, there'll be trouble between the two groups."

For at least half of this dialogue, I use no tag at all. Because only two speakers are involved in this scene, we know that when Gilbert asks a question or makes a remark, the response comes from Cushman. And vice versa. When you engage more than two speakers in a dialogue, it becomes more difficult.

The best pitchers in baseball are constantly changing their techniques because they don't want the hitter to know what's coming. So it is with the writer. Labor to avoid monotony in dialogue; surprise the reader. If you practice this skill, eventually you will find yourself shifting the tag around unconsciously.

Any method, no matter how effective, will grow monotonous if used exclusively. Force yourself to use variety.

III. The Action Tag

Action adds a dramatic touch, and at the same time makes evident the speaker's identity. Examine the following sentence:

William Bradford lifted his head slowly, taking in the group, and asked quietly, "What is your decision?"

What if you remove the tag "asked quietly"?

William Bradford lifted his head slowly, taking in the group. "What is your decision?"

Is there any question at all about who speaks the words? Study the following examples:

Captain Jones bit his lip and smiled. "Ah, that's different!"

Fuller looked haunted, then he sighed and shook his heavy head. "I'm a coward, lass. I just don't have the heart to see the boy go."

Jeff's face fell, and he shrugged. "He'll come around, Mother."

For the sake of variety, place the action at some other position in the character's speech. Or after the character's speech:

"You have been kind. If I should not see you again, let me wish you all good luck." She turned to him and regarded him soberly.

Sometimes I "wrap" the action tags around the dialogue as in the following brief exchange:

Gilbert suddenly was struck with the incongruity of the thing. He grinned widely at Bradford. "No one would believe such a thing. You're a saint—I'm a sinner."
Bradford did not smile. Instead he put his thin hand on Gilbert's wrist. "There was a time when I cataloged men like that—saint or sinner; heaven or hell. But I was wrong." He sighed deeply. "What about you, Gilbert?"

Note that there is no tag to Gilbert's speech, and Bradford's words are "wrapped" or "bracketed" by action tags.
Compare the following two samples:

"Where's Fort Abraham Lincoln?"
"Along that road, four miles to the Point," the driver said.

And with an action tag:

"Where's Fort Abraham Lincoln?"
The driver pointed a finger southwesterly. "Along that road, four miles to the point."

The second has texture, a bit of action that brings it to life.
In one scene from *The Honorable Imposter*, I wanted to highlight the conflict between Gilbert and Humility. Notice how vari-

ety is necessary to make the scene flow:

> She looked at him squarely, and there was a determined set to
> her jaw. Leaning back against the rail, she said, "I'm marrying
> Peter Brown."
>
> "I see." He stood there waiting, for he knew she had taken
> this opportunity to tell him. The ship lifted and fell gently, and
> there was a salty tang in the wintry air. A lantern hanging on
> the mainmast cast flickering gleams over the deck, and her face
> looked like an Indian mask—planed down to simple curves and
> hollows.
>
> "You love him?" he asked finally. He did not miss the quick
> response that swept her face—not disgust, but distrust that
> hardened the soft green eyes.
>
> "I respect him. He's a good man."
>
> "You could say that of Mr. Brewster or Mr. Bradford, I dare
> say. Is that enough for you—respect?"
>
> "It's better than what I got from you!" she cried out, and
> despite her intention to keep her emotions under control,
> anger raced through her as she faced him. "I got *love* from you,
> didn't I? Kisses and promises that made my head swim. Lord,
> what a fool I was!"
>
> He bowed his head, taking the force of her wrath as he
> would submit to a rightful judgment. But he could not let it all
> go.
>
> "All right, I was wrong—I've admitted that. But I want to
> tell you two things, Miss Humility Cooper."
>
> "What could you tell me that I would possibly want to
> hear?"
>
> "When I first met you, it was all a hoax. All I wanted to do
> was to use you." He paused and their eyes locked, and he said
> intently, "But later on, after I got to know you—it wasn't all
> pretense."
>
> She laughed harshly, then said mockingly, "Oh, don't tell me
> that you really fell in love with me! I'm not as gullible as I was
> then, Gilbert!"

He shrugged and said, "All right, think what you will, but I'm telling you the truth. The other thing, Humility, is that even if I am the world's greatest hypocrite and liar, that's no excuse for you to run away from love."

"You don't know what love is!"

"I know one thing—love is not cold!"

A streak of anger ran through him, and he caught her wrist as she turned to leave. "You can't bear to hear the truth, can you? But you're going to hear it this once!"

"Let me go!"

The above scene is primarily dialogue, but I've included enough *action* to keep it lively.

Strive for variety, such as you find in this scene. Some simple "He said–she said" tags, some speeches with no tags at all (especially when the speeches are ones with a fast exchange), some action tags.

The eye and the mind demand variety, so make sure that no single page follows any one method exclusively. A brief series of short exchanges can make the dialogue crackle, but if carried too far it becomes monotonous. The same is true of paragraph-long speeches. Most readers will skip over these to get to the more dramatic forms.

Pacing involves mixing the story elements so that you are constantly leading the reader into new forms—which is one way of keeping him awake! This process requires your deliberate care almost sentence by sentence, and certainly over the confines of a page.

IV. Variety of Length

As you write dialogue, you will find yourself making constant choices. One choice you will have to make continually is how long to make each character's speech. Short? Medium? Long? In *The Fountainhead*, a novel by Ayn Rand, the protagonist makes a speech that goes on for ten pages. It is a series of long paragraphs, each of which often occupies more than a single page.

In Hemingway's novella *Hills Like White Elephants,* a particular scene goes on for several pages in brief monosyllabic speeches:

"Is it raining outside?"
"What do you care?"
"I just want to know."
"No."
"No, *what?*"
"No, it isn't raining."

After about a page of this I lose interest entirely, and after about three of Rand's windy paragraphs, I go to sleep.

How do you know the best pace to use for what you're writing? Sometimes the character's emotions determine the pace. For example, use short, choppy lines when you are recording an argument. You see this illustrated in the scene between Gilbert and Humility above. This is the way people sound when they quarrel. They don't usually go off into long, rambling speeches, though that is possible. But most often it is more of a Snip!—Snap!— Snip!—Snap! sort of affair.

The *sort* of book you are writing can determine the pace. And the kind of person you're writing for—your *reader.* I once wrote a five-hundred-page doctoral dissertation in which I used some extremely long paragraphs. However, I knew only scholars would read it.

But *The Honorable Imposter* is not that sort of book for that kind of reader. It is a historical romance to be read for pleasure. The readers are not expecting long-winded speeches, nor endless pages of stiff expository prose. Look through the book and you will see short speeches and brief descriptive passages. The longest sections are the journals and letters.

In the first chapter, Lady North pins Cecily's character down in a speech:

"You will have your own way, Cecily; your father has spoiled you. But in the end, you will do as I have done. You will consider what is best for your own destiny. Have your fling, but do not make the tragic mistake of throwing yourself away for some romantic dream. You are your father's daughter—and he is a romantic fool. I cannot help *that*. But you are my daughter as well. I know you do not love me, but it is my way you must follow if you are to survive. So—be cautious!"

This may be the longest speech in the entire novel, and I use few of this length. A "medium" speech, then, would be one half this long, and a "short" speech is composed of a single brief reply, sometimes only a single word.

You are in control of the *shape* of your words on the page. When the reader looks at a section of your story on the page, what does he actually see, not *read* but *see*?

In my Zane Grey phase, I quickly learned how to read his novels. If I looked at a page and saw several long paragraphs, I checked the first few words. If they said something like, "The desert was silver in the moonlight... " I *knew* that nothing was going to happen, so I skipped that paragraph. If the next paragraph began, "It was fall, and the snow lurked over the tips of the purple mountains ..." I skipped again.

But when I got to a page with lots of quotation marks—ah! There it was! What I'd been looking for—bullets and bodies!

Readers of popular fiction want to be entertained, and you can only keep their attention if you can offer them a fast-paced book.

V. Tone

We discussed tone in dialogue briefly in unit five, "Character Development—Description and Speech." Here we'll discuss more specific ways to give your characters their own voice.

A. Diction. Each of us has our own stock of words and our own way of stringing them together. Following are two speeches taken from *The Honorable Imposter.*

Speech A

"You would be exactly that, Mr.Winslow, if you spoke so freely to anyone else—but you would be foolish *not* to speak to me. For believe me, I am one of the very few who have the means of getting you out of this snare you have gotten yourself into. But I will not beg. This is my final offer, if you will do as I ask, and give me a complete and thorough account of the period mentioned, I shall—if I am convinced that you are honest—let you know my reasons for being here. Now, I will not add to that. What is your decision?"

Speech B

"That boy stole me tot! See? That's me own ale—and I'll have a piece of 'is skin! Teach 'im to steal from me, I will!"

Do speeches A and B come from the same mouth? Of course not. The first speaker is calm, logical, and self-controlled, obviously an educated man. The second speaker is a rough brute who speaks the language of the deck. Speech A is made by a lawyer named Wellington, while Speech B comes from Jeff Daggot, a bully on the crew of the *Mayflower.*

The ship is crowded with different sorts of men and women, ministers educated at Oxford, merchants from Holland, ignorant bondservants (male and female), a ship's captain, and many others. The educated and cultured character, such as Gilbert Winslow, uses a particular type of speech, while the poor orphan, who has never seen anything but the streets of London, uses another. It is up to the writer to make sure each character sounds authentic.

B. Dialect Dialect quickly becomes tiresome and cumbersome when overused. I wouldn't advise using it with a major character, but I have attempted this device with caution from time to time and find that it can add to the flavor of a character.

In *The Saintly Buccaneer*, Lieutenant Angus Burns from Scotland has a burr in his speech:

"I see nae sense in hauling females on this ship. It's nae guid practice."

"It'll come to nae guid," Burns warned.

"If it's action right away, sir, we'd be hard put to hold our own, as ye weel know."

"I wouldna do that if I were ye, Miss," Burns warned nervously.

As you can see, a few words pronounced and spelled to give the flavor is all that is needed.

In *The Indentured Heart* Molly Burns is also of Scotch blood, but her language in the early section of the book is that of a guttersnipe.

"Oh, please, won't yer tyke a bit of fancy work to yer lady, sir? Yer can 'ave it fer four bob."

This cockney accent would be impossible to bear for long, so I kept Molly fairly quiet until she learned to speak with an American flavor.

Dickens said once, "All fathers have their favorite child—and mine is David Copperfield."

I have a favorite also, and his name is Dooley Wilson. He appears in *The Last Confederate* and is a composite of a number of good ol' southern boys I grew up with in Arkansas. In the section below, he is expressing his admiration for a minister who has just preached a sermon.

"Well, you couldn't have come to hear a better preacher. He's all sorts of a feller, ain't he now? I heard lots of preachin', but that Boone, he really lays it to us sinners, don't he now?"

Thad stared at him, and finally asked, "Are you saved, Dooley?"

"Naw, not yet. But I figger the good Lord's on my trail, Thad, and 'for long I expect He'll tree me like a coon dawg trees a boar coon!"

It is so easy to go overboard with this sort of thing, so that the character sounds like one of the Beverly Hillbillies. Yet, if you do not catch some flavor, a strange thing will happen to your characters:

They will all talk like you!

C. Speech characteristic. This is an expression used often by a character. Dickens used it well. When we hear the words "I will never desert Mr. Micawber!" it can only be Mrs. Micawber.

Dooley says quite regularly, "Ain't that a *caution* now?"

Another speech characteristic might be a mannerism, rather than a phrase. For example, if a character begins every sentence the same way, such as, "Well... "

Or if he stutters slightly: "I c-can't go with you, Richard."

D. Emotional quality. Our characters' emotions should affect the way they speak. Obviously, a quick temper will result in a speech pattern.

"By Harry, haul that windy debate up or knock him on the head!"

No doubt about the temper of the speaker.

If a character is insecure, put that into his speech. Make it halting and jumpy.

"But—I really *can't* go! You know I can't, don't you? I-I mean, what would I *do* there?"

If the character is jealous, let the words reveal it.

"You just *had* to dance with her, didn't you, Gerald?"

These are a few of the things you can do to give flavor to a character's speech. If you can master them and learn when best to use them you will find that your characters will reach out from the page and grab you. And your reader.

Exercises – Unit Seven

~ Exercise 1 ~

Write three character speeches using the following:
A. A quote within a quote
B. A speech that is not completed, that trails off
C. A speech that is broken off abruptly
D. A speech where a question mark is placed *outside* the quotation marks.

~ Exercise 2 ~

Write three sentences containing quotations then rewrite them in *three* ways:
A. Place the tag *before* the quotation
B. Place the tag *after* the quotation
C. Place the tag *within* the quotation

~ Exercise 3 ~

Write a scene one to two pages long, composed primarily of dialogue. Use at least three *action* tags in the scene.

~ Exercise 4 ~

Go over the scene in exercise three and make sure you've used "variety of length": short, medium, and long speeches.

~ Exercise 5 ~

Write half a page of dialogue in which one character speaks with a dialect.

~ Exercise 6 ~

Write three speeches in which the dialogue reveals the characters' emotions.

~

Setting—Elements

Setting refers to the physical elements of the world in which the story takes place. Five of these elements or "worlds" are treated in this unit:

I.   The Geological Background
II. The Weather Factor
III. The Biological World
IV. The Cultural-Historical Flavor
V.   The Social Atmosphere

This list does not exhaust the elements that make up settings, and some of them overlap (culture and social factors, for example), but once you master these five, you can experiment with others. First, we will look at the nature of "setting" and then we will examine each of the five elements more closely.

The Nature of Setting

Novels must have "setting" because they chronicle people's lives, and people must live in a world. Try to picture a great historical figure *out of his setting.*

Can you imagine George Washington wearing Calvin Klein jeans? "No! He wore knee breeches!" we scream. The very idea of Washington in Calvin Klein jeans is offensive, almost blasphemous. Why? Because we think of him only *within the setting of his world.*

What about Joan of Arc water skiing? Or Moses cutting wheelies on a Honda? Henry VIII selling life insurance in Arkansas?

This same thing happens to us when we try to think of great fictional creations. Imagine Huckleberry Finn as a student at Yale. Can you envision Pip and his Great Expectations being moved from the English setting to an African village? Could *Moby Dick* be set anywhere except the sea?

Characters are tied to *place* with steel chains. As Eudora Welty observes, "It is by the nature of itself that fiction is all bound up in the locale... for feelings are bound up in places. Location is the crossroads of circumstance, the proving ground of 'What happened? Who's here? Who's coming?'"

What does all of this mean to you as a novelist?

It means that you must *create* the world in which your story takes place.

If you fail to create a world, your book itself will probably be a failure. As an editor, I often tossed manuscripts in the "Return To Writer" tray because of the writer's inability to create an authentic setting.

Plots do not take place in a sterilized, blank-walled room where two people stand nose-to-nose and talk.

It is your job as the writer to create the steamy room in a cheap hotel on the coast of Guatemala. Or the nuclear sub beneath a mile-thick layer of polar ice. Or the inner city of Detroit where the hero tries to survive a gang war. Huck has his river, Hester has her puritan village, and *your* character has his world.

Sometimes the amateur writer thinks that because he is familiar with his setting, others will somehow (by osmosis, perhaps) sense it as well, but he is mistaken. Remember—your novel's setting will not magically appear, even if it is your personal world.

"I went down and got a hamburger at a fast-food place."

No smell of cooking in that sentence. No golden arches. No little blue packets of sugar. No beat-up Buick taking two parking places. No waitress punching your quarter-pounder, french fries, and small coke into her little computer. It has no *food* in it, no sense of place. "I went down and got a hamburger at a fast-food place." Might as well be on the moon for all the sense of hamburger-ness we get from those words.

How do you put "setting" into your work?

If it is your personal world, you sit at your computer and *remember* what McDonald's looks like and smells like. If it is *not* your world, you find a book that describes the world you want to re-create in your work, and you incorporate what you learn into your story.

Plagiarism!

No—it's called "research." Remember the old joke, "If you steal from one writer, that's plagiarism; if you steal from ten— that's *research!*"

I. The Geological Background

Almost all of the action in some novels takes place inside houses. Others are outdoor novels. *Wuthering Heights* is so tied to the wild moors of Yorkshire that to try to move it indoors would destroy the story.

We live on a thin crust of the earth, drink of its rivers, sail its seas, and climb its mountains. If your novel takes place outdoors, even in part, the reader should get the feel, the texture of that world. In westerns such creation is obvious. A.B. Guthrie in *The Way West* catches the enormous sweep of the western plains in a fine piece of writing:

Evens had heard about the Platte. He had pictured it in his mind. He thought he knew what he was going to see, but now that his horse stood on the summit, he couldn't believe it. He couldn't believe flat could be so flat or that distance ran so far or that the sky lifted so dizzy-deep or that the world stood so empty.... He thought he never had seen the world before. He never had known distance until now. He had lived shut off by trees and hills and had thought the world was a doll's world and distance just three hollers away and the sky no higher than a rifle shot.

What is the single dominant impression of this passage? Size. Scope. Breadth. Now, a passage from Dickens that is just as fine; the coast of the sea, Yarmouth, as seen through the eyes of a child, David Copperfield:

I was quite tired, and very glad, when we saw Yarmouth. It looked rather spongy and soppy, I thought, as I carried my eye over the great dull waste that lay across the river; and I could not help wondering, if the world was really as round as my geography book said, how any part of it came to be so flat. But I reflected that Yarmouth might be situated at one of the poles, which would account for its flatness.... I hinted to Peggotty that a mound or so might have improved it; and also that if the land had been a little more separated from the sea, and the town and the tide had not been quite so much mixed up, like toast and water, it would have been nicer.

The first time I read Guthrie's passage, I thought, *If I could ever write lines like that, I'd be ready to call myself a writer.* But Guthrie's prose is not magic, just fine craftsmanship, and craftsmanship can be learned.

In *The Honorable Imposter*, the pilgrims' first sight of the New World is a discouraging one. They had expected a paradise, but Cape Cod was a cold, bleak, forbidding spot at that time of year. I attempted to capture that dismal sight in the following passage:

The sky was gray as ashes, featureless and stark. Gusts of cold wind swept across the deck, and the shore seemed alien and hostile where it touched the sullen breakers. The harsh cry of a gull seemed an evocation of doom, and there was a brittle, fragile quality about the ship thrown into relief against the eternal whisperings of the sea.

Be as detailed as you can in your own attempt to develop your novel's setting.

II. The Weather Factor

As Mark Twain once complained, "Everybody *talks* about the weather, but nobody *does* anything about it!" As a writer of fiction, you must do something about the weather.

We can all think of exceptions, but most of us write books in which the characters move from inside to outside. In unit nine, "Setting—Uses," we will discuss how to *use* the weather, but in this section, I will simply list the facets of weather and illustrate them briefly from the setting used in *The Honorable Imposter*.

A family of aristocrats must go up the Thames River to get to a ball. "The journey from the palace of Lord North to that of Lord Simon Roth took less than two hours, but it was bitter cold, and the family shivered in spite of the thick furs." In my first draft I used five times this many words describing the biting cold, but cut it to this single sentence. Why mention the cold at all? It is part of the book's *texture*. Even the richest man in all England in 1620 suffered from the weather.

Use weather to get your reader in the mood for something. Just before Gilbert Winslow kisses Humility, a bashful girl, we read: "He walked beside her, and the red flash of the sun threw rippling streaks along the surface of the water in the canal below. The cool breezes of evening brushed against their faces." I needed to slow the action down, and the sun streaks in the water and the cool breeze accomplish this.

"The hot June sun had made a sweltering furnace of the large living room." I wanted the room to be warm and uncomfortable, and weather was the simplest way to gain that end.

Great skeins of tattered clouds were drifting raggedly across the horizon as Gilbert disembarked and made his way along the Southhampton quay.

This is the first sentence of chapter eight, when Gilbert first visits the *Mayflower*. Weather gets this chapter moving.

After getting ashore at Dartmouth, Humility and Gilbert caught the mail coach, then rolled along the Great North Road, huge plumes of dust rising like waves behind them. The fine grains of whitish dust coated them from head to foot, and even the water tasted dusty in the hot July weather.

Does this passage convey heat and discomfort? Make the weather work for you in building *texture*.

A storm gives the writer opportunity to cut his wolf loose. Note the violence of the following passage:

The ship began beating back and forth before the terrible force of the headwind, like an animal running up and down. The light of day failed as the blackness of the cloud wrapped a sable blanket around the plunging ship, and the last flag of daylight, a thin streak of silver-white, was blotted out by the rolling cloud. The dull roaring rose at times to a high-pitched scream, drowning out the creaking of the timbers and the fluttering of the tattered sails.

For effect, hint at the weather to come. In the following sentence, the approaching bad weather is foreshadowed: "A cold wind stung Gilbert's face, and he stared at the rolling water that tossed the long boat like a chip. All morning the sun had been muffled with fat, dark clouds, and even now there was an ominous keening as the winds gathered up and cut across the sea."

In the scene when the *Mayflower* leaves for England, the settlers are cut off completely. I used the wind in the following passage to set off their loneliness:

The women's headcloths flapped in the breeze and the men's

hair and beards ruffled as they sang. Soon only the declining speck of the *Mayflower* could be seen, then nothing broke the flat plane of the wide horizon of the sea.

Cold and hot and wet and dry. Clouds, rain, dust, and sun. Soft breezes and driving winds. These are some of the weapons in your arsenal you can use to create your characters' world.

III. The Biological World

Unless your novel takes place on the surface of the moon, you will create a world covered with plants and crawling with life. Following is a scene from a book I never published. A young boy, Dan, loved the woods and was forced to go live in Chicago's inner city.

Dan trotted up the hill and found the dogs waiting for him, wriggling with pleasure. He gave each of them a quick pat on the head—Little Darlin' with one blue eye and one brown, Julip the biggest with the left ear shredded from an encounter with a boar coon. And his favorite, Dempsey, who could track anything with two legs or four over any kind of ground. He punched Dempsey's solid side with his fist, saying, "Come on, you worthless mutt!" and led them out of the yard, crossing the bare front yard, passing through the pig lot. The huge sow, Cleo, made a quick move toward them, but retreated when all three dogs lifted their muzzles and growled.

An angry fox squirrel chattered as they passed under his territory in the pines and when they passed out of the grove, Dan saw six buzzards circling far off. Finally they passed through the pumpkin patch, and he noted that some were as big as a good-sized orange. By fall the field would be spotted with the orange globes, and his mouth watered as the thought of Aunt Sarah's pumpkin pies suddenly came to him. He leaped a small ditch, scaring a monstrous bullfrog who shot straight up into the air with a hoarse cough and came down in the creek with a splash. He stopped to watch, noted at his feet a tiny purple wild violet, and stooped to pick it up.

In this brief incident, I wanted to describe his world of animals and wild vegetation. Note the details:

Little Darlin' with one blue eye and one brown
Julip with a shredded left ear
Cleo, the huge sow
an angry fox squirrel
six buzzards
pumpkins as big as oranges
a monstrous bullfrog
a wild purple violet

One final illustration, from *The Honorable Imposter*. The pilgrims land and make their first exploration of their new world. As we have seen, it was almost winter, the harsh winter that would kill half of them. To foreshadow the tragedy, I wanted to show the land as hard and hostile, and I used vegetation and a bird to create this impression:

The party turned down a gully where the growth was sparse and proceeded up through the trees. There were evergreens here and there, but otherwise the dead hand of winter had stripped the trees. As they filed across a stretch of marshy ground, a huge crane rose into the air, followed by the quicker flight of a cloud of waterfowl.

There are two types of biological elements—plants and animals. Use them to populate your setting.

IV. The Cultural-Historical Flavor

This division deals with the people who inhabit the cosmos of the novel and the details of their world. Only a piling up of detail will give the reader a sense of the time frame and the particulars of the world in which the characters move.

A. The cultural flavor. In my novel *Delaney*, the setting was Hot Springs, Arkansas. But which *part* of Hot Springs? And *when*? The time is *now* and the part is the world of a police officer. Chapter seven begins with a description of the Hot Springs Police Department as seen from the outside:

> The Hot Springs Police Department is fairly well concealed. It's tucked neatly into a gully on Convention Boulevard behind a gaudy building with an orange sign proudly proclaiming, "BAIL BONDSMAN."
>
> The sloping ground is paved with native stone, so there is no grass to cut. Several architects designed the building, but it was obvious they never met to discuss the plan. One of them designed the roof which is a shabby imitation of early Victorian. The main floor is modern and the basement is a rather sinister gothic—something out of Edgar Allan Poe's lesser stories.

If you ever visit Hot Springs, and drop by and visit the cops, you'll find my description quite accurate. I looked at it and that's the way it is.

What *effect* does this brief description give? That the building is cheap and shoddy. That's the way it is. In descriptions of the inside, the offices and restroom are shabby, too.

In one scene, Delaney enters a bar. I have read enough graphic descriptions to come up with an authentic portrait of what one is like:

> The Red Pony was just about as seedy as most of the other joints in Hot Springs. A lot of blue neon, windows all painted over, local cars nuzzling the white square cubicle just on the edge of the business district. Inside were the usual zombies propped up by a long bar, and people floating around like fish in an aquarium darting here and there to shout intimacies over the din of about a hundred others determined to shout their own. Over all this was the raunchy beat produced by several

hirsute young men wired for sound. There were the electric guitar, bass, drums, all of them making whining noises as if they were in great pain. The young men's faces were twisted into an expression that you ordinarily associate with food poisoning.

A grimy world. That's not the entire world of Hot Springs, but it's the cultural *climate* that Ben Delaney moves in. Following is another example. Anyone who has ever sat in a car on Central Avenue in Hot Springs will recognize this:

A lot of people come to Hot Springs to die. The rich ones hole up in lake houses, but the poor ones you see tottering down Central almost every day. Shapeless old women carrying grocery sacks with who knows what in them. A lot of them dye their hair purple and wear short skirts with elastic garters cutting off the circulation to their fat legs and dimestore rings turning their fingers green. The shattered old men stumble from one position to another as if they were on sentry duty. Sometimes they shave once a week, sometimes not, and the drinkers have little to show for the thousands of dollars they've spent for booze except trembling joints, rheumy eyes, and a good run at cirrhosis of the liver.

You could write a novel set in Hot Springs and present a very different world. Suppose that world revolved around the pastor of a small Baptist church. What would that miniature world contain? Choirs, stained glass windows, deacons, Sunday Schools, Bibles.
Same town—different cultures.
What if your novel were about horse racing? You would have to create the culture of the track—horses, jockeys, Oaklawn, gambling, etc. Another little world in the town called Hot Springs.
If your setting is contemporary, you must fill it with cars, television programs, grocery stores, the local football team, the latest country hit, hula hoops—the thousand small things that, added together, create your cultural climate.

B. The historical flavor. Some things never change; we need

only think of Rip Van Winkle to see that the world moves on and leaves us behind. If you choose to go back in time for your story's setting, you must become an artful archeologist. You must unearth the dress, the speech, the cooking, the rules of courtship of that dead time. Your hero is making his way down a London street in the year 1620. Assignment: describe that street.

Carts and coaches made such a thundering it seemed as if all the world went on wheels. At every corner they encountered men, women, and children—some in the sooty rags of the chimney sweeps, others arrayed in the gold and gaudy satin of the aristocracy, gazing languidly out of their sedans borne by lackeys with thick legs. Porters sweated under their burdens, chapmen darted from shop to shop, and tradesmen scurried around like ants, pulling at the coats of the two men who fought their way through the human tide that flowed and ebbed on the street.

"Watch yourself!" Tiddle said sharply, pulling Gilbert back just in time to avoid a deluge of slops that someone threw out of an upper window. "Nearly got you, lad! But now that the city's put the drain in the street, why every rain will wash away all this garbage." He waved his hand at the ditch about a foot wide and six inches deep in the center of the cobblestoned street. "That carries all the slops and garbage away quite nicely, you know? Wonder what a change modern improvements make, isn't it? Why, most cities just let the garbage and slops pile up—but not London! No, Sir!"

Notice all of the elements that make up the *historical climate* of London in 1620—chimney sweeps, porters, chapmen, coaches. That's the *flavor* of the time and place. The second paragraph surfaces a historical detail in a dramatic fashion; the speaker is *proud* of the central sewage system—a gutter down the middle of the street!

In my novel *The Reluctant Bridegroom*, I wanted to make New

York in the year 1835 real to the readers. In chapter two, the heroine buys some groceries. What did they eat then, and how much did it cost?

The storekeeper was a tall, thin man with a large nose and sharp blue eyes. He touched each item with a boney finger as he called out the price. "Well, now, Mrs. Marlowe, the milk's twopence for the quart, two pounds of beef at sixpence a pound, one chicken for one shilling sixpence, four pigeons at a penny apiece, the pickled herring comes to five pence, and the oysters exactly one shilling."

How did I know the price of groceries at that time and in that place? Research—I got my information out of a book by William E. Woodward, *The Way Our People Lived*.

In that same novel, I describe the woman buying the groceries:

She had come in wearing a blue silk bonnet tied with ribbon under her chin and a sage green cloak which she had set aside to do her shopping. Her bell-shaped skirt, made of dark linsey-woolsey, was stiffened by whalebone sewed into the skirt itself without a hoop. Her green silk bodice was plentifully supplied with lace on the collar and the sleeves. The skirt was not long; it showed about three inches of leg above the shoe tops—a new fashion that had taken New York by storm. Her shoes were delicate high-heeled shoes made of damask.

The historical flavor utilizes clothing, food, entertainment, transportation, architecture, tools, books—all the things that make that particular speck of time unique.

Details bring a scene to life, but at the same time, too much detail detracts from the action. James Michener, with all his fine qualities as a writer, sometimes tells us far more than we need to know or want to know about the background of his stories.

V. The Social Atmosphere

The final element of setting deals with *society*. People live in groups of varying sizes. Use the following classifications as you create your fictional world.

A. The one-person world. Not likely you will rewrite *Robinson Crusoe*, but one of the characters in your novel may be isolated for a time—cut off from society.

B. The submarine world. Many books and novels deal with a small group of people who live together in a society that is isolated from the rest of the world, as in a submarine, for example. The wagon train, the ship at sea, the marooned, the lost patrol—all are of this nature.

C. The small town. The small town differs from the city in more than a census figure. People in small towns think and act differently from those in metropolitan areas, and you must capture the difference in atmospheres.

D. The metropolis. New York, Paris, London, etc. Use specific details to bring these settings to life.

Study published novels for examples of all of the above. I suggest the following:
1. The one-person world—*Robinson Crusoe*
2. The submarine world—*Das Boot* or *The Way West* by Guthrie
3. The small town—*The Hamlet* by William Faulkner or *You Can't Go Home Again* by Thomas Wolfe
4. The metropolis—*Studs Lonigan* by James Farrell

Exercises – Unit Seven

～ Exercise 1 ～

Write a passage which sets the action in the Arizona desert in July at noon. (Obviously the *single dominant impression* will be oppressive heat. Weave a character into the passage, so that your passage will do more than describe.)

～ Exercise 2 ～

Write a scene set in the swamps of Louisiana—way back in the swamp. Let's hear them gators snapping!

⌒ Exercise 3 ⌒

Write a brief scene using two characters. Let the weather reflect the nature of the relationship between the two. Make them angry, happy, sad, afraid, anything you choose, but use the weather to set the tone of their relationship.

⌒ Exercise 4 ⌒

Write a passage which shows a young woman walking across a small field into a farmyard and entering a house. Let the animals she comes across set some sort of mood. For example, her name is Kate and she is lonely. She observes all the girl ducks with their boy duckfriends—ditto the chickens, the cow, the pig. Their companionship is a foil that sets off her own loneliness. (Now, don't write *this* scene!) Imagine how you might use the animals to give color and life to the book and at the same time reveal something about the girl.

⌒ Exercise 5 ⌒

Write a scene in which a mother and her son walk home from the grocery store. They live in an inner city ghetto and inhabit a rat-infested apartment.

⌒ Exercise 6 ⌒

Write the same scene with the mother and son, but set it in Palm Beach, making the mother and son wealthy.

Setting—Uses

Now that you have a grasp on the essence of setting, attempt to master the following five uses of this element in your fiction:

   I.   Create a mood
  II.   Reflect a mood
 III.   Illustrate a moral force
 IV.   Symbolize an idea
  V.   Advance a plot

This list is not an exhaustive use of setting. But master these five, and later you will find other uses for it.

I. Create a Mood

Dickens' *Bleak House* is one of the great *mood* novels. But before you can grasp the genius of Dickens' use of setting to reinforce the novel's theme, you must know what the theme is.

Bleak House reflects Dickens' absolute hatred of the processes of the legal world. His own father had been imprisoned in Marshalsea Prison when Dickens was only a child, and the experience scarred him for life. He became an expert court reporter, and the injustices and delays of the law made him despise the courts and the legal profession to a white-hot heat. There are at least seven plots in the book, and a host of minor characters, but all the elements serve to display English law as the common man's enemy.

It is Dickens' purpose to show that there is nothing clear about the law. Nobody understands it except lawyers, and the poor victim must wander around in a state of perpetual confusion. In the novel a pitiful character named Gridley tells how a simple suit has ruined him:

> My father made a will and left his farm and stock, and so forth to my mother, for her life. After my mother's death, all was to come to me, except a legacy of three hundred pounds that I was then to pay my brother. My mother died. My brother, sometimes afterwards, claimed his legacy. I, and some of my relations said that he had a part of it already in board and lodging and some other things. Now, mind! That was the question, and nothing else. No one disputed the will; no one disputed anything but whether part of that three hundred pounds had been already paid or not. To settle that question, my brother filed a bill, I was obliged to go into this accursed Court; I was forced to go there, because the law forced me, and would not let me go nowhere else. Seventeen people were made defendants to that simple suit! It first come on, after two years. It was then stopped for another two years while the Master (may his head rot off!) inquired whether I was my father's son—about which there was no dispute at all with any mortal creature. He then found out that there were not defendants enough—remember, there were only seventeen as yet! but, that we must have another who had been left out; and must begin all over. The costs at that time—before the thing was begun—were three times the legacy.

One gets the sense of a man caught up in the machinery of a mill, and, unable to free himself, is slowly ground into pieces by a remorseless machine.

Character, of course, carries this theme along, but as I have indicated, every element in the novel does this.

What is the theme, then?

The dark side of the legal system.

How does Dickens use setting to convey this darkness? In a famous piece of prose, he simply describes London—a London buried beneath a heavy, dark fog. As you read the selection below, remember that Dickens is not just filling space. The physical fog that blinds everyone is terrible, but not so terrible as the legal fog that blinds the hearts of the victims:

London. Michaelmas Term lately over, and the Lord Chancellor sitting in Lincoln's Inn Hall. Implacable November weather. As much mud in the streets, as if the waters had but newly retired from the face of the earth, and it would not have been wonderful to meet a Megalosaurus, forty feet long or so, waddling like an elephantine lizard up Holborn Hill....

Fog everywhere. Fog up the river, where it flows among green aits and meadows; fog down the river, where it rolls defiled among the tiers of shipping and the waterside pollutions of a great (and dirty) city. Fog on the Essex marshes, fog on the Kentish heights. Fog creeping into the cabooses of collier-brigs, fog lying out on the yards, and hovering in the rigging of great ships; fog drooping on the gunwhales of barges and small boats. Fog in the eyes and throats of ancient Greenwich pensioners, wheezing by the firesides of their wards; fog in the stem and bowl of the afternoon pipe of the wrathful skipper down in his close cabin; fog cruelly pinching the toes and fingers of his shivering little 'prentice boy on deck. Chance people on the bridges peeping over the parapets into a nether sky of fog, with fog all around them, as if they were up in a balloon, and hanging in the misty clouds.

Gas looming through the fog in diverse places in the streets, much as the sun may, from spongey fields, be seen to loom by husbandman and ploughboy. Most of the shops lighted two hours before their time—as the gas seems to know, for it has a haggard and unwilling look.

The raw afternoon is rawest, and the dense fog is densest, and the muddy streets are muddiest, near that leaden-headed old obstruction, appropriate ornament for the threshold of a leaden-headed old corporation: Temple Bar. *And hard by Temple Bar, in Lincoln's Inn Hall, at the very heart of the fog, sits the Lord High Chancellor in his high Court of Chancery.*

Thus begins *Bleak House*. Dickens was daring to use so many words on fog. But the last sentence explains why he did so: "And hard by Temple Bar, in Lincoln's Inn Hall, *at the very heart of the fog*, sits the Lord High Chancellor in his high Court of Chancery."

Most of us would not dare expand our setting to this extent, but in my detective novel, *Delaney*, the first paragraph works in the same manner. The story is concerned with moral depravity, as all detective novels are. Throughout the novel I tried to show that not all criminals wear stripes, that many of them wear Bill Blass suits and drive Mercedes automobiles. In other words, what you see may be a lie. I attempted to use setting as a means of symbolizing this sad truth:

Most towns are designed by someone who has some concept of traffic flow, but Hot Springs was designed by two lakes—Lake Catherine and Lake Hamilton. They push and nudge at the city, stretching it out like Silly Putty at times, then squeezing it to a ridiculous narrow girth. The shoreline sells for a thousand bucks a foot and keeps going up.

My heart jumps when I look at one of those lovely million-dollar palaces and realize that ten feet under the surface raw sewage is being pumped into the lake. As a matter of fact Lake Catherine was chosen as one of the ten most polluted bodies of water in the nation.

Remember—if the reader is *unaware* of your mechanics, you have succeeded as a writer. Why do some movies hold you spellbound? You are not *conscious* of the background music, or the half-tones of the scenery, or the movement of the camera. It's the *bad* movies that make you notice those things—because the movie fails to hold your attention.

Setting should never be so overdone or garish that the reader thinks, "My, that certainly is a wonderful piece of descriptive writing!" The setting should be like the piers that hold up an elevated highway. When we sweep over the curves at sixty miles per hour, we enjoy the sensation; we do not even think of the pillars underneath us, making our experience possible.

One third of my novel *The Honorable Imposter* is concerned with the life of the pilgrims on the *Mayflower*. I wanted to create the impression of a tiny world, and I mean *world* in a full sense. The little ship *was* a world for them, all they would have until they touched land. In the following lines I tried to convey this concept:

The *Mayflower* was a little world, sailing through the rolling trackless water much as a single star cleaves through the ebony blackness of space. There was a difference, however; the star had fellows (invisible though they were to the eyes), while the ship was solitary.

Bobbing like a cork on the tossing waves, she was smaller than the leviathan that sometimes surfaced close enough for the passengers to see the waterspouts. But though dwarfed by the miles that lay beneath her keel, by the sky that unscrolled blankly over her mainmast, and by the mighty ocean stretching in every direction, she kept a life and order running through the ship—an image of the macrocosm of the planet.

Captain Christopher Jones was the archetype ruler: Master, potentate, king, prince, emperor, congress, parliament, court. He ruled the little world with the power of an absolute despot, the Great Cabin no less the seat of authority than the Vatican or Buckingham Palace.

The ship was its own cathedral, chapel, monastery, nunnery; there were as many divergent views among the inhabitants of the bobbing little world as the babble of tongues in the larger one. From the dim, superstitious thought of Richard Salterne, common sailor, little better than a half-wit, who thought of God only as a sort of murky stew engulfing the earth—to the profound meditations of William Brewster, philosophies of God were as diverse on the little ship as were the staggering varieties of life that teemed beneath her keel.

Make your setting do double duty. The setting is not only a stage for your character, but it also gives the reader a sense of the storm's atmosphere. A gloomy book requires a gloomy atmosphere.

You will make this decision for the overall mood of your novel, but just as the plot and the characters' emotions move up and down a scale, so you will want to adjust your settings to create new moods.

II. Reflect a Mood

Using the setting to *create* a mood is one thing; using it to *reflect* a mood is another. The example from *Bleak House* shows us how to use the setting to cause the reader to respond in a certain way. Dickens wanted us to feel the blindness of the courts and the fearful impotence of those caught up in its remorseless processes.

You can also use setting to reflect a character's mood. Using setting to reflect a character's mood is to give the reader a hint at a character's emotional state of being; whereas in creating a mood, you are focusing on the story's overall tone.

Let's look at two passages from Stephen Crane's *Red Badge of Courage*. The first paragraph sets the tone of the book. It is a dreary scene, a hostile environment that is somehow vaguely malevolent:

The cold passed reluctantly from the earth, and the retiring fogs revealed an army stretched out on the hills, resting. As the landscape changed from brown to green, the army awakened, and began to tremble with eagerness at the noise of rumors. It cast its eyes upon the roads, which were growing from long troughs of liquid mud to proper thoroughfares. A river, amber-tinted in the shadow of its banks, purled at the army's feet; and at night, when the stream had become a sorrowful blackness, one could see across it the red, eyelike gleam of hostile camp fires set in the low brows of distant hills.

Do you see the threatening words—*cold; tremble; mud; sorrow - ful blackness; red, eyelike gleam*? This piece of prose contains just the right tone—a hint of the terrible world of battle that lies just over the crest of the day. The words create a sense of vague uneasi-ness in us as we read them, but we know nothing of the protago-nist's feelings.

The story's theme is courage—or the lack of it. For the first three chapters the young soldier examines himself, trying to deter-mine if he has courage. "Will I run when I get in battle?" is the question he asks himself endlessly.

Finally his regiment goes into battle and the setting becomes a reflection of Henry's thought processes. Almost at once they encounter a dead soldier:

He lay upon his back staring at the sky. He was dressed in an awkward suit of yellowish brown. The youth could see that the soles of his shoes had been worn to the thinness of writing paper, and from a great rent in one the dead foot projected piteously. And it was as if fate had betrayed the soldier. In death it exposed to his enemies that poverty which in life he had per-haps concealed from his friends.

The ranks opened covertly to avoid the corpse. The invul-nerable dead man forced a way for himself. The wind raised the tawny beard. It moved as if a hand were stroking it. He vaguely desired to walk around and around the body and stare; the impulse of the living to try to read in the dead eyes the answer to the Question.

Note two things in this passage. The youth has tried to conceal his fear from his friends, just as the dead man had concealed his thin shoe leather from his friends. And the word *question* begins with a capital letter. What is the Question? It is what all men going into battle wonder about: "Will I run when the battle starts?"

These may seem small things, but Crane uses these tiny fragments like bricks to make a complete structure.

What is the setting of the battle?

As he gazed around him the youth felt a flash of astonishment at the blue, pure sky and the sun gleaming on the trees and fields. It was surpising that Nature had gone tranquilly on with her golden process in the midst of so much devilment.

A beautiful setting, but as the regiment marches on, notice how, *in Henry's mind,* this all changes—the pure sunlight and tranquility is metamorphosed into a nightmarish world:

Absurd ideas took hold upon him. He thought that he did not relish the landscape. It threatened him.... A house standing placidly in distant fields had to him an ominous look. The shadows of the woods were formidable. He was certain that in this vista there lurked fierce-eyed hosts.

Crane *uses* the landscape as a counterpoint to the character's mental and emotional state. And this state is, by the mysterious alchemy of literature, transferred to the mind of the reader.

This is done on film quite routinely. Think about the old classics of horror—*Frankenstein* and *Dracula.* What is the *mood* of these films? A sense of terror—fear of the horrible things that threaten us. And what setting brings this delicious fear into our hearts? Black nights, ancient castles covered with clammy mosses. Dark subterranean passages lit by flickering torches. And the weather! Storms with terrifying bolts of lightning that score the inky darkness, giving us a glimpse of horrible things lurking ahead!

These are gothic scenes and not at all subtle. If you are out to write a gothic novel, draw heavily on this genre—the horror film.

Dickens' *Great Expectations* dips into the gothic mood. The eccentric old lady, Miss Haversham, was jilted by her lover years earlier. She loses her mind and for years has lived in a decaying old mansion. Through Pip's eyes we see this woman's madness. Dickens never *says* she is mad; he is too capable a writer for that. Then how do we know she is insane? The setting reveals this. I will quote at length from chapter eight. First Pip enters the old house which has a true gothic flavor:

> We went into the house by a side door—the great front entrance had two chains across it outside—and the first thing I noticed was that the passages were all dark, and that she had left a candle burning there. She took it up, and we went through more passages and up a staircase, and still it was all dark, and only the candle lighted us.

Finally he is brought face-to-face with the old woman. Read this description:

> She was dressed in rich materials—satins, and lace, and silks— all of it white. Her shoes were white. And she had a long white veil dependent from her hair, and she had bridal flowers in her hair, but her hair was white. Some bright jewels sparkled on her neck and on her hands, and some other jewels lay sparkling on the table. Dresses, less splendid than the dress she wore, and half-packed trunks were scattered about. She had not quite finished dressing, for she had but one shoe on—the other was on the table near her hand—and her veil was but half arranged, her watch and chain were not put on, and some lace for her bosom lay with those trinkets, and with her handkerchief, and gloves, and some flowers, and a prayer book, all confusedly heaped about the looking glass.

Pip's eyes take this in, and for a moment in the half gloom he thinks he is looking at a young bride caught in the midst of packing for a wedding journey. But in the next paragraph we read:

I saw that everything within my view which ought to be white, had been white long ago, and had lost its lustre, and was faded and yellow. I saw that the bride within the bridal dress had withered like the dress, and like the flowers, and had no brightness left but the brightness of her sunken eyes. I saw that the dress had been put upon the rounded figure of a young woman, and that the figure upon which it now hung loose had shrunk to skin and bone. Once I had been taken to see some ghastly waxwork at the fair, representing I know not what impossible personage lying in state. Once I had been taken to one of our old marsh churches to see a skeleton in the ashes of a rich dress that had been dug out of a vault under the church pavement. Now, waxwork and skeleton seemed to have eyes that moved and looked at me. I should have cried out if I could.

I should have cried out if I could, Pip says—exactly the reaction Dickens desires to evoke from the reader. But he is not finished setting the mood, for he quickly directs our attention to the room itself, which like the owner, reeks of death. It is the scene of her wedding feast, and nothing has changed—not since her lover deserted her:

I crossed the staircase landing, and entered the room she indicated. From that room too, the daylight was completely excluded, and it had an airless smell that was oppressive. A fire had been lately kindled on the damp old-fashioned grate, and it was more disposed to go out than to burn up, and the reluctant smoke which hung in the room seemed colder than the clearer air—like our own marsh mist. Certain wintry branches of candles on the high chimney-piece faintly lighted the chamber, or, it would be more expressive to say, faintly troubled its darkness. It was spacious, and I dare say had once been handsome, but every discernable thing in it was covered with dust and mould, and dropping to pieces. The most prominent object was a long table with a table-cloth spread on it, as if a feast had been in preparation when the house and the clocks all stopped together. An epergne or centre-piece of some kind was in the middle of this cloth; it was so heavily overhung with cobwebs that its form was quite undistinguishable; and, as I looked along the yellow expanse out of which I remember its seeming to grow, like a black fungus. I saw speckled-legged spiders with blotchy bodies running home to it, and running out from it, as if some circumstance of the greatest public importance had just transpired in the spider community.

I heard mice too, rattling behind the panels, as if the same occurrence were important to their interests. But, the black beetles took no notice of the agitation, and groped about the hearth in a ponderous elderly way, as if they were short sighted and hard of hearing, and not on terms with one another.

I can never read the words, "speckled-legged spiders with blotchy bodies running home to it," without feeling the most unpleasant sensation. The spiders, the mice, the roaches, the mould, the darkness—all of it is a symbol of Miss Haversham's diseased mind, but it is also Dickens' way of baptizing the reader into the eerie state of that mind.

Not all moods are gloom and doom. The classic passage in *Huckleberry Finn* that describes life on a raft, for example. The novel is set on the Mississippi River, and two worlds are in conflict, the peace of the river and the busy world of men and civilization. Every time Huck leaves the raft and goes into the world of men, he gets into trouble. The society there is filled with violence and deceit, and it is only when he returns to the raft that he feels a sense of peace. The following passage reveals Huck's thoughts about life, his philosophy (though he would never call it that) of life. It offers a stark contrast with the clamor of civilization:

We said there warn't no home like a raft, after all. Other places do seem so cramped up and smothery, but a raft don't. You feel mighty free and easy and comfortable on a raft.

This is the *philosophy*, the rest of the passage a dramatization of that philosophy. Only a man familiar with the river, such as Mark Twain was, could have written it so well.

Two or three days and nights went by; I reckon I might say they swum by, they slid along so quiet and smooth and lovely. Here is the way we put in the time. It was a monstrous big river down there—sometimes a mile and a half wide; we run nights, and laid up and hid daytimes; soon as night was most gone we stopped navigating and tied up—nearly always in the dead water under a towhead; and then cut young cottonwoods and willows, and hid the raft with them. Then we set out lines. Next we slid into the river and had a swim, so as to freshen up and cool off; then we set down on the sandy bottom where the water was about knee-deep, and watched the daylight come. Not a sound anywhere—perfectly still—just like the whole world was asleep, only sometimes the bullfrogs a-cluttering, maybe.

Sometimes we'd have that whole river all to ourselves for the longest time. Yonder was the banks and the islands, across the water; and maybe a spark—which was a candle in a cabin window; and sometimes on the water you could see a spark or two—on a raft or a scow, you know; and maybe you could hear a fiddle or a song coming over from one of them crafts. It's lovely to live on a raft.

It's lovely to live on a raft. This passage gives us a micro-world—the world of the river. Twain's purpose is to contrast the quiet peaceful world of the natural with the harsh violence that jars Huck's soul in the world of commerce and greed.

Your job is to create a setting that reflects your fictional world. The readers of modern fiction demand this, even though they may not know what it is or how it works. Now we move to another function that setting performs:

III. Illustrate a Moral Force

Most fiction is concerned with the morals of mankind. Even atheistic writers are constantly telling us by word or action in their works that something isn't fair. But as C.S. Lewis so admirably proved, if there is no God, there is no such thing as *fair* or *unfair*. Hitler is no "worse" than John the Baptist unless a line is drawn somewhere between "right" and "wrong."

About half the Ph.D. dissertations over the last few decades were entitled "The Moral Vision of 'Somebody'." And your writing will have a moral tone. John D. MacDonald's hard-nosed sleuth Travis McGee had not one trace of traditional Christian value in him, still he held certain things to be "right," and we can assume that these were the things MacDonald himself felt were worthwhile.

The whole question of how to present moral insights in the fiction form without turning the story into a sermon is complex, but I want to show you how you can use setting in your fiction to impart a moral force.

The following scene is taken from my novel *Delaney*. The protagonist goes into a bar, and as he looks around he meditates on the scene:

I guess there may be a sadder sight somewhere than the scenes that roll on endlessly inside these small bars all over the country, but offhand I can't think of any. Huddling in the darkness, there they are, the misplaced persons of our emotional culture. The bunnies are ravenous for romance, yet settle for what they call "making out." The futile acne-pitted men drift out of high school into a world so surfeited with unskilled labor there is a competition for the sacking jobs at Safeway. Somewhere they must have had at least a hope that if you are sunny, cheery, sincere, group-adjusting, and popular, the world is yours, a world of barbecue pits, diaper-service, percale sheets, friends for dinner, and the home projector. But it all gets lost or sidetracked into a den like this—a murky cave filled with losers. I've read about underground rivers where fish lose their eyes, trapped so far from light, and I never step into one of these bars without thinking that somehow I've stepped into some sort of murky cavern far away from all that's good and wholesome—so far away that those who grope in the watery darkness have lost all traces of a moral vision.

I've taken the second example from *Oliver Twist*, a novel of blinding contrasts. The child Oliver arrives in London and falls into the hands of Fagin, a monstrous old man who runs a school for young thieves. The following gives the detailed setting of Fagin's abode:

The walls and ceiling of the room were perfectly black with age and dirt. There was a deal table before the fire: upon which were a candle, stuck in a ginger-beer bottle, two or three pewter pots, a loaf and butter, and a plate. In a frying-pan, which was on the fire, and which was secured to the mantelshelf by a string, some sausages were cooking; and standing over them, with a toasting-fork in his hand, was a very old shrivelled Jew, whose villainous-looking and repulsive face was obscured by a quantity of matted red hair. He was dressed in a greasy flannel gown, with his throat bare; and seemed to be dividing his attention between the frying-pan and the clothes-horse, over which a great number of silk handkerchiefs were hanging. Several rough beds made of old sacks were huddled side by side on the floor. Seated round the table were four or five boys, none older than the Dodger, smoking long clay pipes with the air of middle-aged men.

The above is a brilliant mixture of character development, description, and setting. The silk handkerchiefs are important, for in the next chapter we find that Fagin gives lessons to the boys in the art of picking pockets. The entire passage gives us the microcosm of the world of thieves, and it is not overdone (something that Dickens has been known to do). An air of evil hangs over the house, and gross sin in every form thickens the very air.

Oliver is arrested, but instead of being deported or jailed, Mr. Brownlow takes him to his home. He is ill at first, but when he recovers he finds himself in a world as different from the world of Fagin as the earth is from the surface of the moon:

> They were the happy days of Oliver's recovery. Everything was so quiet, and neat, and orderly; everybody so kind and gentle; that after the noise and turbulence in the midst of which he had always lived, it seemed like Heaven itself.

Read the entire section of *Twist* to see how Dickens uses setting to illustrate the moral worlds that Oliver moves between. In Fagin's world, sin and crime and vice exude from the grimy settings, while at Mr. Brownlow's home, the simple virtue of the good man and his family are a counterpoint to the dignity, quietness, and peace of the house they inhabit.

IV. Symbolize an Idea

In the 1840s James Fenimore Cooper wrote novels which revealed Americans as a people of courage and virtue, a people who could meet any challenge. Nationalism was sweeping the new nation, and Cooper wanted to dramatize the New American for the world to see.

What setting did he choose? His most successful work was the Leatherstocking Series, based on the adventures of a man called by many names: Natty Bumppo, Deerslayer, Leatherstocking, etc.

For a setting, he chose that dark wilderness that stretched from the Ohio River to California. It was a dangerous world filled with wild beasts and wilder Indians. The stories of Deerslayer take place against this setting. He becomes king of this wild world and assumes mythological strength and power.

In one sense, you could say that the wilderness, the setting, is the most dramatic character in the book, for it is a *symbol* of the challenge that man must overcome. This taking of the world to symbolize a force or idea is widely used in literature. The sea in *The Old Man and the Sea*, the desert in *McTeague*, the river in *Huckleberry Finn*, the city in *Studs Lonigan* just to mention a few.

For illustration purposes, let's look at *Typee* by Herman Melville. In the eighteenth century an idea surfaced—the convention of the noble savage. This idea stated that the pure and beautiful child of nature was vastly superior to the civilized man. He was the center of a nostalgic dream of pastoral serenity, a green Tahiti of the soul in a world of growing industrialization and complexity. Reduced to a formula, this idea would read: *civilization spoils men, so what we must do is get back to nature.*

This idea still lurks in the American mind. Every generation brings a wave of "Back to the Land" movement; the present preoccupation with the past is a splinter from the board.

Now, Melville did not believe in the noble savage. He believed that a savage was no more noble than a mill hand in Bristol, that virtue was not built into a jungle paradise any more than it was in a shipyard. *Typee* was his statement of this to the world.

One way he accomplishes this is through *setting;* the first part of the story takes place on board *Dolly*, a whaling vessel.

Dolly represents the mean, disgusting world of civilization. Law aboard *Dolly* is "the butt end of a handspike, so convincingly administered as to effectively silence the aggrieved party." Men are reduced to whining servility and treachery. Life's necessities and luxuries are scant or nonexistent. Food is stale, water is stale, life is stale.

The nature of humanity on board *Dolly* is dramatically portrayed when a group of young native girls swim out and come aboard ship. They are noble savages, innocent in the ways of the civilized world:

All of them at length succeeded in getting up the ship's side where they clung dripping with brine and glowing from the bath, their jet-black tresses streaming over their shoulders, and half enveloping their otherwise naked forms. There they hung, sparkling with savage vivacity, laughing gaily at one another, and chattering away with infinite glee.... What a sight for us bachelor sailors!

The expected occurs, and the narrator says sadly:

Our ship was wholly given up to every species of riot and debauchery. Not the feeblest barrier was interposed between the unholy passions of the crew and their unlimited gratification. The grossest licentiousness and the most shameful inebrity prevailed, with occasional and but short-lived interruptions, through the whole period of her stay. Alas for the poor savages when exposed to the influence of those polluting examples! Unsophisticated and confiding, they are easily led into every vice, and humanity weeps over the ruin remorselessly inflicted upon them by their European civilizers. Thrice happy are they who, inhabiting some yet undiscovered island in the midst of the ocean, have never been brought into contaminating contact with the white man.

The last sentence highlights the ship as the symbol of civilization itself. The entire novel turns on this, for in the next section two sailors, Toby and Tommo, jump ship and make their way to an island filled with natives who have never seen a white man.

So Melville, having created a symbol of the corrupt western world on the ship *Dolly*, must now create another world—the world of the noble savage. For chapter after chapter he writes of the mild climate, the beautiful natives, the abundant fruit and verdant vegetation, the streams and lakes that sparkle like glass. He sums up the idyllic life of the two white men:

There were none of those thousand sources of irritation that the ingenuity of civilized man has created to mar his own felicity. There were no foreclosures of mortgages, no protested notes, no bills payable, no debts of honour in Typee; no unreasonable tailors and shoemakers, perversely bent on being paid; no duns of any description; no assault and battery attorneys, creating discord, backing their clients up to a quarrel, and then knocking their heads together; no poor relations, everlastingly occupying the spare bed-chamber, and diminishing the elbow room at the family table; no destitute widows with their children starving on the cold charities of the world; no beggars; no debtors' prisons; no proud and hard-headed nabobs in Typee; or to sum it up all in one word—no Money! "That root of all evil" was not to be found in the valley.

Melville goes to infinite trouble to create an Eden—and then he rejects it. Eden is beautiful; the world in which man actually does live is a nightmare of misguided politics, sterilizing technology, brutalized law—but hideous as it is, it is the world in which humans *develop*.

He points out that the noble savage can *become* nothing. He aspires to nothing. He makes no plans. He has no great dreams. His life is that of an animal, he seeks contentment only. Melville's use of setting to symbolize his idea that man must not retreat into a monastery or to a desert island but win his soul in the world of civilization is a stroke of genius.

V. Advance a Plot

Setting can move the action along. You can use it as a chronological tool. In *Huckleberry Finn*, the river is the measure of time. Huck moves five miles down the river and has an adventure. A week later, he moves ten miles further and has another and so on to the end of the book. The river setting ties the plot together.

The seasons mark the passage of time, and the action is flagged by red, falling leaves, or spring flowers, or driving winter snow. *Across Five Aprils*, a novel for young people, uses the setting of the

Civil War. The entire war is laid across the span of this novel, and the reader can never get lost chronologically.

Remember—you must have character and action, but it's possible to write a book without weather, dirt, snakes, and sidewalks. Don't do it! Make setting work for you.

Exercises – Unit Nine

⌒ Exercise 1 ⌒

Write a scene set in the world of business. Create a *cold* world where the individual does not matter. There is no warmth in this world, and only one issue—profit. It is a hard, unemotional world where survival of the fittest is the norm. What would a normal human being feel? Probably despair, as in Orwell's *1984.*

⌒ Exercise 2 ⌒

A young man is leaving home for the first time. The character arrives at a place that fills him with great happiness. He's *glad* to be there, away from home. Write the scene.

⌒ Exercise 3 ⌒

Rewrite the scene above. The character leaves home and arrives at a place that fills him with disgust or fear or despair. *In these two exercises, it is the setting that creates or reflects the character's emotional condition.*

⌒ Exercise 4 ⌒

In this chapter, I used a scene from my novel *Delaney* to show how a setting can trigger a character's moral judgment. Write a passage in which the setting impacts the character positively or negatively; cause either a good or evil force to dominate the setting.

⸻ Exercise 5 ⸻

Use a setting to symbolize an idea. Take, for example, the idea that man is killing himself by destroying the planet. A character could go fishing at a spot where he'd caught good fish before, only to find dead fish floating on the surface, killed by pollution. The setting itself symbolizes the idea; the character need not speak at all.

⸻ Exercise 6 ⸻

List five ways you can use setting to advance a plot. Give examples.

Sample: Spatial. For example, a character could travel across the country, so that the highway is the medium. He stops in one state for a time, then moves to the next state.

Marketing Your Writing

My friend Joe is a fine dramatic actor. I met him when he was a student at the university where I taught. He dominated the stage, and his burning ambition was to be a professional actor. After he graduated his last words to me were confident. "It will be tough and competitive, but I'm going to make it!"

He went at once to New York and plunged into the world of professional theater. We kept in touch, and his letters were always hopeful. I watched him once or twice in small television roles, and was certain that he possessed the talent and drive to make it in a highly competitive profession.

Finally he returned home for a visit, and in our first conversation he told me his story.

"I'm exhausted," he said. He had lost weight and had a harried look in his blue eyes.

"Is professional acting so much harder than amateur?" I asked.

"Oh, it's not the acting," he assured me. "I can go for hours on the stage and never run down."

"Well—what is it then?"

He shook his head and for the first time I saw defeat and confusion in his face. He said finally, "It's the things you have to do to get to act—that's what's ground me down."

"What kind of things, Joe?"

He spread his hands wide and shook his head again. "Well, begging for a chance to work, I guess. I spend most of my time sitting in some agent's office. Usually there's a lot of us, and when I get in, I'm just one more face. I have to *convince* him that I can do the job. But I'm not a *salesman*, I'm an actor!"

He told me how most of his life in New York had been like that. Getting a résumé together for a certain role, going from office to office, waiting most of the day, then getting shuffled off so the producer could get through the line of hopefuls, going home night after night with nothing to show for the effort, and feeling a little grimy after the struggle.

"I know I can do the job," he told me with tears in his eyes. "But it looks like nobody is going to give me a chance to prove it!"

I realized at once that Joe was caught in a terrible trap, a trap that most artists have to endure. Artists are usually "un-worldly" people; they are more interested in their art than they are in anything else. But the people involved in the marketing of art are very worldly!

"Will it *sell*?"

That's the question looming in their minds, and that's how they evaluate the artist and his work. It makes a difficult situation for the artist or writer or actor.

The artist is a sensitive person and wants to perform, or paint, or write. But if he is to survive, he must have a market. So he is forced to do something which is foreign to his nature and repugnant to his spirit.

He must become a salesman. He must put his painting under his arm and go from gallery to gallery, hat in hand, and humbly request that they buy his paintings. The actor must bow and scrape before agents and producers. And the writer must send his work to publishers.

An English lady named P.D. James wrote a book and sent it off to a publisher. It was accepted and became a best-seller almost instantly. She wrote another; same result, another best-seller. At this time she has written nothing but best-sellers and has never gotten a rejection slip in her life.

This is not going to happen to you. Every writer has to submit manuscripts to publishers—and none of us like it. Most of you do not write for yourself alone; you write for readers. The painter wants others to enjoy his pictures and an actor wants to perform for an audience.

No matter how well you write, your work will not feel complete until you are in print and people are reading what you have written.

In order to get into print you must master the following "non-artistic" principles:

   I.   **Philosophy of Writing**
   II.   **Knowing the Market**
   III. **Preparing a Manuscript**
   IV. **Writing a Query Letter**
   V.   **Sending Your Work**

I. Philosophy of Writing

The word "philosophy" sounds heavy, and many of the books with this word in the title are boring enough to stun an elephant. I have a doctorate in philosophy and have waded through enough of this sort of thing for one lifetime. I have no interest in subjecting you to such a traumatic experience.

But aside from the technical use of the term, there is a more practical aspect of philosophy.

A. You can control your behavior through your personal philosophy. If you are not satisfied with your *behavior*, you can change it by changing your *philosophy*. The two most able soldiers in the Continental Army during the Revolution were George Washington and Benedict Arnold. Military historians are divided as to which of them was the most able general. But what a difference in their lives. One laid everything he had on the line to save his country, while the other sold his sword to the enemy for cash. Why did they behave differently? They had two different philosophies. Washington said, "My country is the most important thing in the world. I'll do anything, suffer anything to save it." Arnold's philosophy was, "I am more important than the cause of the Revolution." The two men behaved according to their sharply differing philosophies.

The Bible says plainly, "Keep thy heart diligently, for out of it are the issues of life."

This ancient principle is like the law of the Medes and the Persians which changeth not. Men and women *act* out of impulses that they have built into their inner systems. Someone has said, "We are what we eat," and physically that may be true. But it may be closer to the truth to say, "We are what we have decided to become."

Now let's apply this to ourselves as writers. I have seen this principle demonstrated in my students for years. Two students of relatively equal ability sit in the same classroom. They have the same text, the same syllabus, the same professor; one of them makes a D and the other makes an A. Why? Because they have different philosophies. A's attitude is, "I'm a good writer, but there are thousands of good writers around; therefore, I'm going to have to work hard at being accepted." D has the philosophy, "I am a good writer, and it's up to someone to *discover* me."

B. You are doing a worthwhile and valuable work. A critical question to ask yourself as you're developing your personal philosophy as a writer is: Why do I want to write? Motives for writing are many and varied:

"I want to make money."

"I want recognition and admiration."

"I write because it's what I *like* to do!"

In one way, the above are all selfish motives, goals that would bring us pleasure, that would benefit us personally. That doesn't make them wrong. But there is some danger if goals like this are *all* that motivates you to write.

History is cluttered with the lives of those who lived only for themselves, those who gained it all, only to discover that what they gained was not enough. Financial rewards are fine, but there is a part of us that wants more than that.

In our time all has gone to the marketplace, but great poets have always insisted that the written word had a power beyond the denotative. Wordsworth, Shelley, Keats, all saw themselves giving to the world in their work something therapeutic.

Only a few days ago, a local college librarian said to me, "Dr. Morris, your *House of Winslow* books are the most popular books on our shelves. They are checked out more than any other books."

It took me aback, and I answered, "That's not good, is it? Doesn't it show that the scholarly level of the students is fairly low when historical novels lead the list?"

He grinned. "I don't think you need to worry about that. The students tell me they study the *hard* books until they're exhausted. Then they check out one of your books and it rests their minds to read something light that doesn't take a lot of thought."

I take that as a compliment. That's what the *House of Winslow* novels are designed for; light reading with a little Christian flavor and a touch of romance. They are not designed for scholars to pore over with red-lidded eyes but for people to enjoy.

I began writing Christian novels because I saw a gap in the market. I liked science fiction, detective novels, westerns, and most of the stuff I encountered on the bookshelves was not suitable.

Why do you want to write? If it's only for money, you may make some. If it's to get attention, that may come, too. But if those are the only things you want, there's something lacking.

"I want to do something good." That sounds puritanical to the modern ear, but I trust that you feel like that. Beyond the money and past the recognition, I hope your philosophy, or one pillar of it, includes using your voice to help the world.

One more aspect I want to touch on. As Henry David Thoreau

remarked, "The mass of men lead lives of quiet desperation." Millions of people put in eight hours a day doing something they hate, so they can get off work and do something they like. If this is multiplied, it means that they work at something they despise for sixty-five years, so that they can finally retire and do what they've really wanted to do all along.

Most of us have to work, but blessed are those who are able to do that which they love as their means of support.

Cliff Harris, a student of mine, left our college and went without being drafted to the Dallas Cowboys as a safety. He played in several Super Bowls and was All-pro safety for several seasons. I never will forget what Cliff said after his first professional game: "Gosh! I can't believe they're going to *pay* me to play football! I'd play for *nothing*!"

Robert Frost's poem, "Two Tramps in Mud Time," has a line in it that has haunted me for years:

My object in living is to unite
My avocation and my vocation
As my two eyes make one in sight.
Only where love and need are one
And the work is play for mortal stakes,
Is the deed ever done
For Heaven and the future's sake.

If you have talent, and if you will put in the hours and not give up, you can make it as a writer. You can do what you really want to do, and that's something that most people miss in this brief life.

C. You will survive rejection. One thing about your life as a writer; you *will* meet with rejection. Your success as a writer will probably not depend on how well you write so much as in how you handle rejection.

When I went to study for my doctorate years ago, it didn't take me long to see that I was the dumbest student in every class. Most of the other students had gone to prestigious schools and were able to answer the professor's questions when I couldn't even understand the questions. I remember handing in those first papers. Mine all came back looking like they'd been in a bad accident and with a large *F* at the top. I was ready to run for the hills.

But I had a year's leave of absence so I stayed. I floundered along as best I could, trying to keep a low profile so the professors wouldn't notice me and humiliate me by asking one of those awful questions I couldn't understand.

I passed all the course work somehow, struggled through two languages, and then it was time for the prelims. I had to pass them in a number of areas, such as Medieval literature, the Renaissance, Modern American literature, etc.

By the time they came up, I was accustomed to just putting my head down and trying, no matter how unlikely it seemed that I would pass. So I met them head on and passed them all.

But a strange thing happened to many of my fellow students, those who had known all the answers in class, who'd gotten the A's while I was fortunate to get a low B.

I first noticed it when one of my friends didn't take the Eighteenth Century prelim.

"Why didn't you show up for the test, Marie?" I asked.

"Oh, I thought I'd study a little more," she said carelessly. "I'll take it in the fall."

"But you've had all the courses," I protested. "You couldn't miss!"

"Oh, sure, but I just thought I'd wait."

As far as I know, Marie is still waiting. She didn't take the test in the fall, and when I left she was still waiting for a better time. And she wasn't the only one. Many who had been at the university long before I got there were still "waiting until the fall," or "until I have another course or two," or some other excuse.

Do you know why they wouldn't take the prelims?

They were afraid of failure.

As long as they refused to take the tests, they were safe. They could say, "Why, of course I can pass the prelims!" But if they took them and failed, it took away their excuse.

That is why many writers never succeed.

They write a piece of work, then hesitate. "Maybe I'll do one more rewrite," they mutter. So they fiddle with it, and three months later they steel themselves to the act of submission to a publisher, but they say, "More research! Yes, that's what this piece needs! It would be accepted, no doubt, but I want it to be perfect!"

No, they don't want that. They want to protect themselves against the day the envelope comes back with the enclosed letter that says, "Thank you for letting us see your work, but at this time we cannot accept it."

I wish I could communicate how minor it is, the receiving of a rejection slip. But it seems to be one of those things which can be caught but not taught.

After I wrote *Delaney*, my first detective novel, I sent it out with high hopes and flags flying. I wondered what I would do with all of the money that would soon roll in. I planned the conversation with my boss with delicious anticipation: "Oh, yes, Dan, I won't be able to help you out next semester. Love to, but just too many writing commitments, you know how it is."

Well, about a month later, *Delaney* came rolling home, a form rejection slip on top.

Was I crushed? Yes.

Was I disappointed? Certainly!

Did I think the publisher who rejected me was nuts? Sure of it!

Did I cry? On the inside, yes.

Did I quit? NO!

I typed another letter, put it on top, and shipped it off again.

And a month later it came back.

So I wrote another letter, put it on top, and shipped it off again.

I went through this twenty-eight times!

And the twenty-ninth time Wendall Hawley, Senior Editor at Tyndale House, wrote me a letter. It was only one line long:

"If you can finish this novel to our satisfaction, we would be interested in publishing it."

It had taken nearly a year, but I had finally found a publisher who would take my work.

At this point, I have no idea how many rejection slips I've acquired. I'm sure I could paper the walls of a good-sized auditorium with them.

But they don't hurt any more. I've learned one thing about rejections; they don't mean you're not a good writer. In the past six years I've published twenty novels through four very good publishing houses. But I still get rejections.

A rejection slip can mean any number of things. It can mean that the publisher doesn't take that sort of work. Or that the publishing house recently signed a contract for a book just like yours. It can mean they're about to go under and aren't taking *any* work. It can mean that the editor was having an emotional crisis on the day your manuscript arrived and was in no condition to give your work serious consideration.

As I said above, the important thing to keep in mind is that a rejection slip is not a measurement of your writing ability.

D. Believe that you will make it as a writer. I am not qualified to teach anyone how to learn to believe in himself. And I'm not sure that anyone really is.

What I am certain of is that some people have a gift for writing. If you are one of those people, how did it get there? I believe God put it there. For what purpose? To be used for his glory.

Of course, not all writers write for the glory of God, just as not all singers sing for his glory. But if you know that God has given you this talent, and if you are willing to develop it, then you can move in a spirit of faith.

If you want to be a writer, you've got to believe in yourself. And as I've tried to point out, you will have a difficult time. You're going to get rejections. Some will tell you to quit.

And many writers do just that.

But I want to encourage you not to let difficulties or discouragements stop you. A friend of mine, Lowell Simmons, had terminal cancer when he was seventeen years old. "No hope," the doctors all agreed. But Lowell believed in divine healing. He began praying and asking God to heal him. He went down physically, and almost everyone gave up. It looked like the end had come. One of his friends said, "Lowell, it looks like you're not going to be healed. Just give up."

Lowell said, "No! I may die of this thing, but if I die, I'll go in faith believing God will heal me!"

God did heal him, and he has had a tremendous life. He is a man who knows how to believe—and hang on.

As a beginning writer, I learned something about faith from my friend: "I may never get anything published, but if I die, I'll die believing that my books will get in print!"

I still think like that, though I have experienced some success. I have yet to attain all of my writing dreams. But I'm going to! It may take time and sweat and tears and postage and rejection slips high as a house, but I'm going to make it.

This is not a pep talk to get your emotions charged up. We can't let emotion control us, especially the kind of heavy gloom and despondency that can come with rejection or failure. We must learn to write in the middle of that, just as football players must learn to play with pain.

These are the words that you want to repeat as often as is necessary: "I am a writer, and I'm going to be a better writer, and I'll die believing that!"

II. Knowing the Market

If you have taken any writing courses, read any books on writing, or attended any writing workshops, you will recognize this principle. In order to sell your work, you must understand how the market works, so you can get your manuscript into the hands of the right publishers.

If a man suddenly came into possession of a number of specialized wrenches, it would do him little good to go door to door, asking, "Would you like to buy some nice metric socket wrenches?" Oh, he could conceivably hit a mechanic who might be interested, but not likely. He would do much better to go around to automotive shops, for that is where the men work who use wrenches.

At some point in your writing career, you may have to put in almost as much time finding markets and sending off manuscripts as you spend on the writing itself.

As a matter of fact, unless you are tremendously successful in the manner of Stephen King or P.D. James you will always spend *some* time in this area.

And although you can always discover new wrinkles, the science of locating and analyzing markets is not difficult once you understand the process.

A. Master all the obvious markets. First and foremost, buy a current copy of *Writer's Market.* This thick volume lists the most widely known markets for all types of fiction. Be sure to purchase the new edition when it is released each year. The markets change quickly. Publishing houses fail or change their emphasis. Since new markets are included in each new edition, it's well worth the twenty bucks you'll invest.

Using *Writer's Market* is simple. It is divided into obvious sections: Book publishers, Consumer publications, trade and technical journals, greeting card publishers, etc. Every edition includes the section "How to Use *Writer's Market.*"

Find the section that fits your need and wade through it. For example, if you've written a romance novel, you will find a page which lists all the fiction markets. This page is subdivided into types, so that you can pinpoint specific kinds of fiction markets without having to scan all the book publishers listings. Now, simply go down the list of publishers until you find romance.

If you turn to the first listing, Arbor House, you will discover that this company is interested in "Quality fiction—everything from romance to science fiction, fantasy, adventure and suspense."

The second entry on the list is Atheneum Children's Books. When you turn to that listing, you will discover that this firm wants all types of fiction, but "all in juvenile versions."

Do you see how these market listings can help you focus on the best publishers for your novel?

Several other books (most of them sold by Writer's Digest Books) list markets even more specifically:

Children's Writer's & Illustrator's Market
Novel & Short Story Writer's Market
Poet's Market
Songwriter's Market

These books often list specialized markets you won't find in *Writer's Market*.

The second major tool in finding markets for your work is *Writer's Digest*, a monthly guide to getting published. This periodical is designed to help you find new markets and tips on getting published. Subscribe to it at once. You will pick up something in every issue which will be of help.

B. Keep searching constantly for fresh markets. The publication of novels is such a massive undertaking that new publishing houses do not often spring up overnight. But new magazines do. In every new edition of *Writer's Market* you will find many new publications listed. An even more current list of these will be in the current copy of *Writer's Digest*.

You have a much better chance of selling a short story than a novel, especially before your name is known to editors. Every writer should have several short stories circulating as they are good training for writing longer works. And an acceptance from time to time gives the struggling writer a real boost. A list of credits builds your confidence and gives you something to put on your résumé. And publishers pay attention to it.

This is basically the way to study the markets. I have spent many hours plodding methodically through page after page of listings in *Writer's Market*. There are no short cuts. It may not be "artistic" work, but it is a part of every writer's life.

II. Preparing a Manuscript

This is one facet of writing that requires no particular originality or creativity—just a few fundamental rules to follow. As a matter of fact, resist the urge to submit your manuscript on lavender colored paper or in orange envelopes. These tactics immediately alert the editor that you are an amateur. Observe the following fundamentals carefully and you will be safe:

A. Use white paper that measures 8 1/2 by 11 inches. A good 25 percent bond holds up well, shows type neatly, and is excellent for editing.

B. Use a decent sized font and avoid fancy script. Dot-matrix printers have been improved, but they are still far from letter quality. Get the printer that you can afford. The ultimate, of course, is the laser printer.

C. Maintain a margin of one and one fourth inch on top, bottom and sides. Begin the first page of a short story or of a chapter in a novel one third of the way down the page.

D. Number your pages. If you can, use a running header or footer that gives the chapter number as well as the page number on each page.

E. Place your name, street address, city, state, and zip code on three single spaced lines in the upper left corner of the first page and at least your last name or the novel's title on each succeeding page.

F. Make a copy of your work. Keep your original as a file copy. Use it to make your copies, and inform the publisher if you are sending multiple submissions. Some firms will not accept material submitted simultaneously, and they may assume that a photocopied submission is simultaneous. Your personal computer may generate copies more cheaply than you would pay to have them returned. If so, simply enclose a self-addressed stamped envelope with your submission and inform the publisher that you don't need the manuscript returned, but you would appreciate a response in the small envelope.

G. Only send manuscripts on disk, or by modem or fax when specifically instructed to do so by the publisher. You must be certain that your computer will match the publisher's. If you see the phrase *query for electronic submissions* in the publisher's listing, you can probably work something out—*after* sending your work and attaining the publisher's permission.

H. Always include a SASE with your work. Self-addressed stamped envelope, that is. This is rule number one. It is also rule number two, three, four, etc. And the "stamped" part of this formula doesn't mean a single stamp. If your manuscript has thirty pages, find out the cost of mailing it. Once you know the cost, put it on both the outside envelope and the SASE.

IV. Writing a Query Letter

The query (or cover) letter is your introduction to the editor and an important part of marketing your manuscript.

This morning I sent a manuscript to a publisher in San Diego. Their entry in *Writer's Market* states: "Publishes twelve to fifteen titles a year; receives 2,500 submissions annually."

This means my chances that they will publish my novel is one in two thousand? A long shot indeed!

Imagine that you are sitting in the editorial office of this firm. The mail arrives, and at each of three desks, the editorial assistant drops a stack of bulky envelopes and cartons. Look at the editors—one is a twenty-year-old woman named Debbie, one a forty-five-year-old man named Les and the last is an elderly lady named Edna. Does it matter which editor gets your manuscript?

Absolutely! Edna may read your work and see at once that it's *just* what the world needs. Debbie may read it and be turned off at once.

What can you do to be sure you get the best reader?

Nothing.

Well, I've done *one* thing. I've sent the manuscript back six months or a year later, hoping for better luck in the draw.

So, back to the editorial room and the desk where your manuscript sits. On this desk are three boxes. The largest is marked "NO." Already the stack of rejected manuscripts reaches well over the reader's head.

Another box is marked "MAYBE." It contains a few manuscripts that have made the first cut and will be passed along for further study after which they will land on the Senior Editor's desk.

The third box is marked "YES."

And what is in the third box?

Usually not much.

I hate to mention this, but there is the chance that your manuscript will not even get a reading. Sad, but true. Editors often have more work than they can do, and there's no way to guarantee that your manuscript will be read.

The best you can hope for is to make it to the MAYBE box. But you first have to avoid the NO box. This is where the query letter comes in. How well you write it may determine where your manuscript ultimately lands.

Now, under certain circumstances, a query letter written by Moses himself wouldn't help your case. For example, if the firm simply does not publish the type of manuscript you've submitted, you are doomed. It's too late to pray! All of my books have a Christian flavor, so would I send a manuscript to the American Atheist Press in Austin, Texas? What do you think they would do with it if I did? Player's Press in Studio City may be an excellent firm, but in their listing they state plainly, "No novels are accepted. We publish plays only." I once spent a lot of money and time submitting manuscripts to inappropriate markets, and I want you to avoid that pitfall.

Back to the office again. The man named Les has picked up your manuscript. As he lifts it out of the box, he makes several assessments:

Well, at least there's an SASE! He places that on his desk, then glances at the manuscript.

Pretty good looking manuscript. And the pages are numbered ...

You have just passed one hurdle. You did not irritate the editor by inflicting a second-rate manuscript on him.

Now, Les studies the query letter.

Aside from the quality of the work itself (an element, the importance of which can't be minimized), this letter offers you your best shot at staying out of the NO tray.

Three things you should *not* say in this letter and Les has heard them all more than once.

1. Resist telling him how hard you've worked on the manuscript. He is not at all interested in how much work you put into the novel, so his eyes automatically skip sentences like: "I spent five years researching this book." That means nothing to Les.
2. Refrain from claiming divine inspiration. When I was editor of *Christian Poetry Journal*, at least half of the submissions that crossed my desk began with "God gave me this poem ..." If your work is truly divinely inspired, let it speak for itself.
3. Repress the urge to tell Les how *wonderful* your work is. That's exactly what *he* must decide, and no eloquence on your part is going to sway him.

"Well, what *can* I do?" you ask.

You can do the following:

A. Keep your letter brief. A single-spaced one-page business letter is best. Do *not* address an editor by a first name.

B. State the nature of your submission. Writers are tempted to explain, to defend what they have written before the poor editor even knows *what* is being explained. I mailed a proposal to InterVarsity Press this week. I let the editor know exactly what I am asking him to read in my first paragraph:

> "The spectacular success of Frank Peretti's *Darkness* novels have proven that there is tremendous public for this genre. I have written a novel, *The Mirror World*, which is similar to Peretti's work, but differs sharply in several respects."

Whether you are submitting an article to *Dairy Goat Journal* on a new method of feeding goats or a novel to Doubleday, state the nature of your work clearly and at once.

C. Use a strong opening to catch the editor's interest. "But you just said to open the letter with a simple statement of what the book is about."

Yes, but sometimes you might want to take a chance, use a clever opening. Just be sure it's clever and creative, not silly.

D. Mention the market you want to target and why your novel is better than others of the same nature. In the first paragraph of my letter to InterVarsity Press, I mention the market, those who like to read about spiritual warfare. Following is my effort to show the editor that my book was different (better) than those already on the market.

> "I wanted to write a book that stressed the terrible conflict that men and women have with demonic powers, but I did not want to put it in the realm of the physical. That isn't really the way it happens, is it? We struggle with thrones and dominions, but in prayer and the spirit. In any case, I think that *The Mirror World* avoids that physical manifestation of demons and deals with the struggle that goes on in the heart, deep down in the inner man."

The query letter cost about as much blood, sweat, and tears as the novel itself.

E. Give your credentials for writing the piece. Include all publications to your credit, but if you have none, that's OK. If you're writing a novel about a nurse, tell the editor you've worked as an RN for ten years. If your novel is set in New Orleans, and you've worked on a newspaper there for five years and know every crooked politician in the parish, go ahead and say so.

Following are three sample query letters. They are custom-made for markets that I am trying to reach.

SAMPLE QUERY ONE
(For a children's novel, ages 8-12)

James Taylor, Book Editor
Imperial Publishing House
1445 Elm Street
Chattanooga TN 56120

Dear Mr. Taylor:

The enclosed manuscript, *The Tree Rustlers Mystery*, is the first of a series of children's novels, "The Double-decker Series," ages eight to twelve. The plot centers around the family of a minister who converts an English double-decker bus into a motor home which becomes a rolling parsonage. Each book takes place in a different locale—the first in the Ozark Mountains, the second in a fishing village in Maine, etc.

The four children range in age from eight to sixteen, and each book deals with problems of growing up. Each book also has some sort of "mystery" that is solved by the children.

What adds most to this proposed series is that the children are home-schooled. The home school movement is exploding in this country—no publisher has issued any fiction aimed at this new market. I have spoken to many home schoolers, individually and in groups, and the one thing they all voice is: "We can't find enough good fiction to keep our kids busy!"

This series could be a forerunner in that market (which does not mean, of course, that it cannot be marketed in bookstores with success).

If you think this series is a possibility for your firm, I will be happy to send you a full manuscript of *The Tree Rustlers Mystery.*

Sincerely,
Gilbert Morris

SAMPLE QUERY TWO
(A fantasy novel aimed at the youth market)

Ms. Amy Funderburk, Editor
Academy Press
1059 No. 8th. Ave.
Dallas TX 10220

Dear Ms. Funderburk:

Charles Dickens once remarked: "Like many fond parents, I have in my heart a favorite child—and his name is *David Copperfield.*"

I have published twenty-nine novels in the past six years, but I would have to say that my favorite "child" is the one I enclose— *Captain Chip of the Rag-Tag Brigade.*

When I wrote it, I thought of the market who made up the readership of *Watership Down* or *Wind in the Willows.* Books that I loved as a boy—and books that I still love at considerably more years!

I send it to you because of your successful record of publishing books of this nature. You publish many books that are romantic, visionary, or have imaginative quality, often with a mythic feeling where fantasy and reality coexist. I think *Captain Chip* falls within these lines.

If you would like to see the complete manuscript, I will be most happy to send it at once.

Sincerely,
Gilbert Morris

SAMPLE QUERY THREE
(A detective novel)

Ms. Mary Hughes, Senior Editor
Green Willow Publishing House
1232 Lincoln Ave.
Atlanta GA 12221

Dear Ms. Hughes:

The field in Christian fiction is getting a little crowded, but one field has not been tapped.

There are no Christian detective novels to be found on the shelf.

Dani Ross is a detective—beautiful and intelligent. She comes from a long line of lady detectives, and the secular market is getting all of them. I am convinced that Christians read mysteries. I know that at least *one* of them does!

Dani Ross is enrolled at seminary, planning to be a missionary. When her father has a heart attack, she is forced to leave school and return to her home in New Orleans to take over until he recovers. She soon discovers that all the high theology she learned at seminary doesn't work too well on Bourbon Street in the French Quarter. To make it worse, the street-wise ex-cop she hires, Ben Savage, is convinced that a woman's place is home with the kids! Dani sets out to prove that a Christian can function in the grubby world, and as the danger mounts, Ben is forced to re-think his ideas on women.

There is a series in this book, I feel sure, and if you are interested in seeing the complete manuscript, I will mail it at once.

Sincerely,
Gilbert Morris

The last letter got an immediate reply from Revell Publishers—and now you will find six *Dani Ross* mystery novels on the shelf.

V. Sending Your Work

Even nonhunters have heard of such a thing as "buck fever." The would-be hunter practices with a fine rifle until he feels sure of hitting his target. He gets outfitted at the local sports store with the latest in fashionable hunting clothes. He obtains a license from the court house. On the first day of the season, he is on the stand, ready and waiting. After a few hours, he hears a sound to his left. Without moving a muscle, he shifts his eyes and sees a ten-point buck step into the clearing not more than thirty feet away.

Slowly he swings the rifle into position, *very* slowly so that he will not startle the buck. He finally gets the bead right on the heart—and then something happens. He begins to tremble; the rifle wavers off the target. He finds suddenly that he *can't pull the trigger!* The buck bounds off leaving him a mass of quivering frustration. He will relive that scene a thousand times.

Buck fever—when the work and the waiting is done. All you have to do is pull the trigger.

But many writers get a bad case of buck fever when it's time to send the manuscript to the publisher.

They get everything ready, but find that they just must do a *little* more fine-tuning on the book. "I don't feel good about chapter three. It needs a bit more research."

Loosely translated that means, *"I've lost my nerve!"*

The root of the problem is the simple fear of rejection and failure. But as I said at the beginning of this unit, these two things are an organic part of a writer's life, maybe of everyone's life.

But with a writer, it's different than, for example, the mechanic who goes to work every day, does his job, and goes home. A writer sinks his life into a novel or story with no promise of a paycheck. Most likely, he's defied convention by quitting a steady job to write or else pounded it out in the evenings or on weekends.

Now he must submit that part of his life to what seems a cold and unfeeling process. An editor in New York or Boston holds his future, and he has no influence over that editor.

You're tempted to protect yourself. "If I don't send it, they can't reject it," is the stubborn thought that you may never speak but that you must acknowledge.

If you don't send it, they may not reject it, but also, it will never get published.

I have a few suggestions:

A. Send your work to market as soon as it's finished. In one way, it will *never* be finished. Something could always be reworked, some passages could be improved. But some writers fiddle with their material to the extent that they make it worse instead of better.

Be firm with yourself. "It's not perfect, but it's the best I can do right now!"

Learn to slam the lid on a piece of work and move on to the next project.

B. Send your story to several publishers at the same time. This is perfectly permissible as long as you are honest. Let each publisher know that you've sent the manuscript to other firms. If their listing says, "No multiple submissions," play fair.

C. Send a minimum amount of material. Send a query letter, three sample chapters, and a brief summary of the plot. The only exception to this is when the publisher asks to see the complete manuscript.

D. Keep a careful record of your submissions. Unless your memory is better than mine, you will forget what, who, and when. What did I send? Who did I send it to? When did I send it?

Every writer should have a dozen things in the mill. One friend of mine keeps over a hundred articles going the rounds.

When I was a young man, I would trot-line in the river. You stretch a heavy line across the river, then attach short lines six feet apart each with a hook on the end. You bait the hooks, then go back to the fire and swap lies until it's time to run the lines.

If you've got one hundred hooks out, how many chances do you have to catch a fish? Why, one hundred! And with fifty hooks you've got a chance at fifty.

What if you only put *one* hook on the trot line?

I sent off eleven manuscripts this week, all novels of one kind or another. Guess what will happen in about a month.

First, my manuscripts will start reappearing in the old mailbox. I'll recognize them because they'll come back in my self-addressed stamped envelopes.

But it only takes one acceptance to change the whole picture. And with eleven manuscripts out, that's likely to happen.

I went though this about six months ago. I mailed out thirty manuscripts.

Twenty-nine of them returned with a nice rejection slip attached, but I received an acceptance: a contract to write a series of detective novels for a major publisher.

The above is my approach to the submission of manuscripts. This is what works for me. Other writers have other methods. Some writers carefully structure their submissions to only a few publishers. Rather than taking the shotgun approach, they spend much time on a single proposal with one publisher in mind. These writers feel comfortable with this method.

Many writers have agents who submit their work for them

which leaves them free to spend all of their time creating. This is especially true outside of the Christian publishing industry. If you can find an agent to represent you, do so. Another possibility is that someone in the publishing business will recommend your work. If you know a successful writer or editor, ask for help.

E. Keep your material moving. I keep submissions in a special file. In each file are three chapters of the novel (usually the first three), a brief plot summary, and a history of that particular book's publishing record. These are my originals. If a submission returns worn or smudged, I run off another copy, add the query letter, record where it's headed, and turn to a fresh project.

I want to say, "Don't sit on the mailbox." But I do quite a bit of mailbox sitting myself, so all I'll say is, "It's *much better* if you can forget the submission and work on something else." However, hope is a thing with feathers that crouches in the soul, so we'll probably both keep on mailbox perching.

As I mentioned at the beginning of this book, writing is like juggling—you must keep many balls in the air at the same time.

You've just received a crash course in the fundamentals of writing fiction. I hope I have helped in the mechanics of writing—just knowing how to handle the machinery of fiction. But I wish even more that I could help you emotionally. I mean by that, I hope you catch fire. It's one thing to teach you how to write dialogue, but even more important and fulfilling, I want to see you go past what I've taught, to become a writer!

God speed you on this way!

Order Form

#	Title	Price	Total
	Just Write—Susan Osborn	$12.00	
	A Complete Guide to Writing for Publication—Susan Osborn	$15.00	
	How to Write and Sell a Christian Novel—Gilbert Morris	$12.00	
	Write His Answer—Marlene Bagnull	$12.00	
	An Introduction to Christian Writing—Ethel Herr	$17.00	
	SUB-TOTAL		
	+ S&H*		
	TOTAL		

*S&H: Add $4.00 shipping and handling for the first book and $1.00 for each additional book.

Purchase these books from your local bookstore or contact:

Write Now Publications
5501 N. 7th Ave, #502
Phoenix, AZ 85013

800-931-BOOK (2665)